STUDY SKILLS
FOR COMMUNITY
AND JUNIOR COLLEGES

STUDY SKILLS
FOR COMMUNITY
AND JUNIOR COLLEGES

Walter Pauk
Director, Reading Research Center
Cornell University

RESTON-STUART Publishing Company
P.O. Box 4067   Clearwater, Florida 33515

Printed in the U.S.A.

Library of Congress Catalog Card Number: 87-060317

ISBN: 0-9614487-1-7

CONTENTS

Chapter 11   Building Your Vocabulary   97

Chapter 12   Research Papers   111

Answer Key to the Multiple Choice Quizzes   125

PREFACE

Performance, not promise, is the key to your success in college. College is no place for the procrastinator, the big talker, the goof-off, or the uncommitted. Positive action is essential and this book is a great place to start. It's filled with suggestions for improving the way you study. So, don't just read about these study methods; try them out! Many will work for you. Some may not. The only way to find out is to take action.

But, action must not be of the hit-or-miss variety. No, it must be systematic. Systematic techniques are the backbone of every chapter in this book; thus, enabling you to stand tall and work smart.

HERE'S A BIRD'S EYE VIEW OF THE CHAPTERS IN THIS BOOK:

Achieving Success (Goal Setting) You won't get there, unless you know where you're going. Setting goals is not kids' stuff. Business executives at all levels are required to set goals continually.

Concentration Without concentration, there can be no learning. With it, almost anything is possible. The five great concentration tips, including the spider technique, found in this book, are bound to make you a better concentrator.

Remembering In college, the big job is remembering. To aid your memory, we arm you with four powerful techniques: recitation, categorization, mnemonic devices, and mental visualization.

Notetaking You'll fill dozens of notebooks in college. Notetaking is the best way to capture each course's information. We offer you the most widely used system in the world: the Cornell System.

Classroom Lectures   There's more to notetaking than scribbling. You need to know how to listen meaningfully, record notes efficiently, as well as, heed warnings against taking notes in shorthand or taking them on tapes. Also, we present new ideas on taking notes on lectures given via TV.

Textbook Assignments   Above all, you must be able to master the textbook. To do so, we offer you the SQ4R System, as well as, tips such as, marking the textbooks, making notes in the margins, reading prefaces and introductions.

Putting Your Notes to Work   With piles of lecture notes and textbook markings on desk, now what? You must commit them to memory. How? By using the powerful recitation method, which is fully explained in this book.

Objective Tests   "I know my stuff, but I still do poorly on tests." Perhaps we can help you. Here's a long chapter that gives you the inside story on how to take the following four tests: True-False, Multiple-Choice, Matching, and Sentence-Completion. Also, we give you the procedures to know when to guess and when not to guess.

Essay Tests   "Essay tests throw me!" They shouldn't. This chapter will teach you how to get "psyched" up for an essay exam, what to do before you answer any question, what the content of your answer should be, how to identify and interpret key words in the questions, plus many other hints for taking essay-type tests.

Vocabulary   Right or wrong, you are judged by the words you use. Pronounce them correctly and use them in their right places with precision, and you'll be judged an educated, clear-thinking person.
Yes, knowing your job is important, but you need more than this to make it to the top. Dean Trembly makes this point clearly: "Aptitudes will give you a good start, but it takes vocabulary to keep you going. Don't wait too long to start working with words."

Research Papers   It's easy, once you know how to do the following: choose and narrow your topic, provide a focus for it, do the library research, organize your notes, rewrite and edit your paper, and finally fine tune your paper's technical details. All these steps and more are thoroughly covered in this chapter.

1
ACHIEVING SUCCESS

What does it take in order to be successful in school?   You need three things: a goal, a plan and an action.

YOUR GOAL

Do I really need a goal in order to be successful?

A goal is an essential component of success. It behaves like a ship's rudder, steering you along on a straight, time-efficient course. So determine what your goal is and then write it out.

Do I have to actually put my goal on paper?

Yes. When you write out your goal it forces you to think about it more precisely than you would if you just kept it in your head. In addition, if your goal is written out, you can refer to it from time to time--for inspiration.

Inspiration?

That's right. Although a goal appeals to reason, it appeals to the emotions as well. For example, the motto "Pikes Peak or Bust" was no magic carpet, but it made the blazing sun and dusty trails more bearable for America's pioneers. It somehow pulled wagon after wagon through. Your goal can have a similar effect.

Finding Your Personal Goal

If you're having a tough time pinpointing your goal, the following exercise may help.

1. On a piece of paper write down your major activities followed by the reason or purpose for each.

2. List the things that you are not presently working on but would like to have or do.

3. Now look at the things that you've written down. Is there any one item which seems to stand out as being the most important? Locate that item and write down its importance to you. Be honest. Nobody has to see this but you.

4. The last answer should have helped to give you any idea of what you really want in life. Is your goal any clearer now? If so, write it down and keep it in mind always.

YOUR PLAN

Is a course plan a good idea?

Yes. A course plan can be a great way to track your progress as you move towards your academic goal. There's a real sense of accomplishment each time you put a check next to a class that you've completed.

What other plans will help me to get organized?

The best plan for getting better organized is the time schedule. No one gets any special treatment as far as time is concerned. A time schedule is a solid plan which should allow you to make the most of the precious time you have.

Should I write down my time schedule as well?

Like a goal, a written time schedule is a record of your expectations. But unlike the goal, the time schedule is actually a step-by-step procedure for meeting those expectations. Once the schedule is put on paper it seems to have an energizing effect; that is, since you made it and planned it, you feel that you control your time, and not the other way around.

I really value my free time. Isn't a time schedule going to interfere with that?

On the contrary, with a time schedule, you'll know just when you're supposed to be working and when you're not. As a result, free time will really be *free* time. You'll be less apt to feel guilty during those times when you are taking a break from study.

What should my schedule look like?

There are three basic types of time schedules, all of which I'd recommend. The first is called **master schedule.** It lists all the unmoveable essentials in your day, such as classes, meals, sleep and any work commitments. It can be drawn on a regular-sized sheet of paper that has been divided up into days of the week and hours of the day. The master schedule should be drawn up once a semester and used as a basic framework.

My classes begin and end at odd times. Should I still divide my master schedule into time blocks that begin and end on the hour?

Yes. Trying to make up a schedule with blocks that begin at odd times will only serve to confuse you. Your master schedule isn't intended as a super-precise chart. Instead, it should be thought of as an illustration which shows you at a glance which time blocks are committed and which are free for study and recreation. So, if your class begins at some time other than on the hour, write it in where it belongs and then draw a box which will approximate its start and finish time.

What's the second type of schedule?

That's the **detailed weekly schedule.** It picks up where the master schedule leaves off. In fact, it would save time if you made several copies of your master schedule. Then, at the beginning of each week you can fill in the gaps with the activities that you have planned for that week. Figure 1.2 provides an illustration of a detailed weekly schedule based on the master schedule in Figure 1.1

Do you have any tips for organizing my own schedule?

Yes. Here are a number of suggestions which should help to make your schedule-planning go smoothly.

Figure 1.1   A Master Time Schedule

	Mon	Tues	Wed	Thurs	Fri	Sat	Sun
7-8	← Dress and Breakfast →						
8-9	Psychology	English Comp	Psych.	English Comp.	Psych.		Dress and Breakfast
9-10							
10-11	Intro Computer		Intro Computer		Intro Computer		
11-12		German II		German II			
12-1	Lunch	Lunch	Lunch	Lunch	Lunch		
1-2							
2-3	management Seminar		mgmt. Seminar	Psych Lab	mgmt Seminar		
3-4							
4-5							
5-6							
6-7	← Dinner →						
7-8							
8-9							
9-10							
10-11							
11-12	← Sleep →						

Tips for Schedule-Planning

1. **Get rid of "dead hours"**--No time block is too small for you to accomplish something.

2. **Use daylight hours**--Research says that daytime study is 33% more efficient than study at night.

3. **Study before discussion and/or recitation classes**--It's best to keep material fresh in your mind in any class in which you may be called upon to speak.

4. **Study after lecture courses**--You'll retain more from a lecture course if you review your notes right after class.

5. **Don't make your schedule too detailed**--Efficiency is important, of course, but a schedule that is too tightly packed will be tough to follow.

6. **Try to study in one hour blocks**--50 minutes of study with a 10 minute break has been found to promote optimum efficiency.

7. **Make room for meals and sleep**--Skipping needed food and rest may seem to save you time at first but in the long run it will adversely affect your health as well as the quality of your education.

Is the third type of schedule shorter?

Yes. **The daily slip schedule** is a small piece of paper or file card on which you have listed the "things to be done" for the following day. Unlike the master or detailed-weekly schedule which should stay home on your desk, the daily slip schedule works best if it is kept handy in a shirt pocket or purse.

When should I write out this slip?

The best time for writing out your daily slip is right before bed. By then you will know exactly what work has been accomplished and what still needs to be done.

I'd rather not have to worry about the next day just as I'm falling asleep.

You won't. The daily schedule will prevent worry, not promote it. There'll be no need to fret about tomorrow's responsibilities. Everything you have to remember will be there when you need it, on your pocket-sized card. When morning comes you'll rise with the feeling of "There's work to be done. Let's get going! As a result, you'll be more vigorous and dynamic, both physically and mentally. What's more, you'll

Figure 1.2   A Detailed Weekly Time Schedule

	Mon.	Tues.	Wed.	Thurs.	Fri.	Sat.	Sun.
7-8	←——— Dress and Breakfast ———→						
8-9	Psychology	English Comp.	Psych.	English Comp.	Psych.	Study Computer	Dress and Breakfast
9-10	Study Psych	Study English	Study Psych	Study English	Study Psych		
10-11	Intro Computer	Study German	Intro Computer	Study German	Intro Computer	Study German	
11-12	Study Computer	German II	Study Computer	German II	Study Computer	Swimming	
12-1	Lunch	Lunch	Lunch	Lunch	Lunch	Lunch	
1-2	Study Mgmt.		Study Mgmt		Study Mgmt		
2-3	management Seminar	Work on English Paper	mgmt. seminar	Psych Lab	mgmt Seminar		
3-4							
4-5	study computer	Study Psych	Study Computer		Study Computer		
5-6	←——— Swimming ———→						
6-7	←——— Dinner ———→						
7-8	Study Mgmt	Study German	Study Mgmt	Study German	Study Mgmt		English
8-9	Study Computer	Study Psych	Study Computer	Study Psych	Study Computer		Paper
9-10	Review Mgmt	Review Computer	Review Psych	Review German	Review English		Study Psych
10-11	←——— Recreational Reading ———→						
11-12	←——— Sleep ———→						

(Sat. column, vertical: Church, Recreation, Conversation, Special Projects, Reading, Extra Work on Difficult Subjects, Thorough Review)

(Sun. column, vertical: Church, Recreation, Conversation, Recreational Reading) feel as though you are in control of your time and your life, and not the other way around.

What does a daily slip schedule look like?

Figure 1.3 provides you with a pretty good example.

Any other advice on making up a schedule?

Here's a hint: For the majority of students, the weekend is a total loss as far as study is concerned. Few will deny that the weekend is prime time for recreation. However, for those students who swear off study as soon as their last Friday class ends, the weekend closes on a sour note with some stressful last minute study on Sunday night. This situation can be avoided with a minimal amount of study throughout the weekend.

Making the Most of Your Weekend

FRIDAY: Make this night a weeknight and you'll still have time for fun after the work is done.

SATURDAY: Don't sleep in. Get up at the regular time and put in a few hours of study before lunch time. When afternoon rolls around you'll be ready for some guilt-free recreation.

SUNDAY: The day is free until dinner time. After dinner, put in a few hours of work catching up, going ahead or conducting a relaxed review.

TAKING ACTION

Won't a goal and a time schedule be enough to bring me success?

Will a rocket sketched on a piece of paper fly you to the moon? Of course not. You have to build it first and it has to work. Many of us have goals and plans. But it's the people who take action that make their dreams come true.

By taking action, do you mean performing?

Yes, performance, not promise, is the key to your success. College is no place for the procrastinator, the big talker, the goof-off or the uncommitted. Positive action is essential and this book is a great place to start. It's filled with suggestions for improving the way you study. So don't just read about these study methods. Try them out! Many will work for you. Some may not. The only way to find out is to take action.

Figure 1.3   Daily Slip Schedule

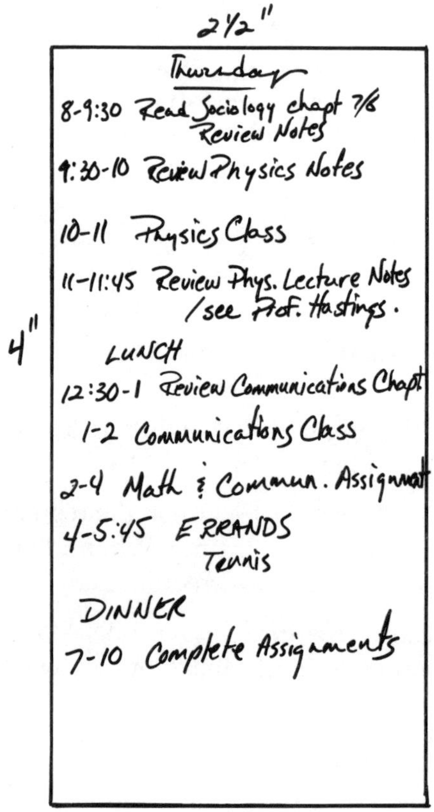

MULTIPLE-CHOICE QUIZ

1. In order to be successful you need
    a. a goal.
    b. a plan.
    c. action.
    d. all of the above.

2. The best plan for getting organized is
    a. a self-help book.
    b. a clean desktop.
    c. a time schedule.
    d. none of the above.

3. Research shows that the most efficient study comes
    a. before class.
    b. after class.
    c. during the day.
    d. at night.

4. It is best to try to study in time blocks of
    a. one hour.
    b. two hours.
    c. ten minutes.
    d. twenty minutes.

5. No matter how busy your schedule becomes, you should always make time for
    a. visiting friends.
    b. taking short naps.
    c. math and science.
    d. meals and sleep.

6. The daily schedule should be written
    a. first thing in the morning.
    b. right before bed.
    c. during lunchtime.
    d. whenever you have a chance.

7. In order to make the most of your weekend you should try to put in some studying on
    a. Friday evening.
    b. Saturday morning.
    c. Sunday night.
    d. all of the above.

8. Even the world's most efficient time schedule is useless without
    a. action.
    b. photocopies.
    c. detail.
    d. "dead hours."

9. A master schedule should be made up
    a. once a day.
    b. once a week.
    c. once a semester.
    d. once a year.

10. A time schedule can increase your overall
    a. assignments.
    b. guilt.
    c. efficiency.
    d. time.

2
LEARNING TO CONCENTRATE

How important is concentration? Extremely important. Put in simple terms, concentration is thinking. Therefore, if you want to think effectively, you must concentrate. Unfortunately, concentration possesses a slippery quality which makes it difficult to maintain.

What do you mean? The moment you notice you're concentrating, you're no longer concentrating! To truly be concentrating you must think only of the task at hand.

What breaks concentration? Any sort of distraction can disrupt your concentration. These distractions can be either external or internal.

EXTERNAL DISTRACTIONS

What do you mean by external distractions? External distractions are any outside stimuli which undermine your concentration. That can mean sounds, sights, smells and even something as simple as a blunt pencil point. Below you'll find a list of suggestions for beating these external distractions.

Combating External Distractions

Find a good place to study.
Use a comfortable chair.
Keep all materials close at hand.
Have good lighting.
Avoid noise.

Where to
Study

Is the library the best place to study?   Probably, although it can depend upon the library. Some libraries turn into active social centers. If that's true of your library then it's probably better to stay at home, that is, if you plan to get any work done. Generally though, you can't beat a library for uninterrupted silence.

But aren't little noises more distracting when they occur in a quiet place?   It's true that isolated whispering in an otherwise quiet library can sometimes be more distracting than constant noise. However, that does not mean that you should seek out a study area which features steady noise. *Any* distraction is going to rob you of the mental energy that you should be reserving for studying. A constant drain on your mental energy is going to be worse in the long run.

The Right
Desk Chair

Isn't a straight-backed chair better for keeping you alert?   If you ask me, that's a myth. Some people argue that a cushioned chair is going to make you tired. My response is that a straight-backed chair is going to make you uncomfortable. This discomfort can be more damaging than fatigue. Besides, as you will see later on in the chapter, fatigue is seldom the result of a padded chair.

Proper
Equipment

How will keeping materials close at hand help my concentration?   The answer is simple: Any time you have to get up to find a paper clip or some extra paper or to sharpen a pencil you're going to have to break your concentration. If everything you need is in reach, there'll be no need to interrupt your thinking.

Lighting

What constitutes good lighting?   Experts tell us that you need three qualities in order to have good lighting: no glare, no high contrasts and no flicker. You can avoid the problem of glare by using a shade (most lamps come with them, of course) and by bouncing the light (off a light-colored blotter, for example) instead of looking directly at it. The best way to remedy high contrast lighting is to have a second light source which will wash out any shadows that are caused from the first. Finally, you can eliminate flicker by using a two-tubed lamp if you favor fluorescent light or simply tightening the bulb if you work under incandescent light.

Which type of light do you prefer?   I go for fluorescent light. Here's why. Traditional incandescent bulbs give off an orangish twilight sort of glow while fluorescent light is more of a broad daylight blue green. As a result, fluorescent light helps to give me a wide-awake feeling even if I have to work late into the night. I further improve my light source by using a drafter's lamp. The adjustable arm allows me to move the light closer or further away as I see fit.

Would you consider music noise?   Technically, while you're studying, any unnecessary sound can be distracting. That includes music. No matter how pleasant it may seem, it's still diverting your attention from the work at hand.

Do you recommend ear plugs?   Disposable ear plugs are a popular item at some community and junior colleges. They're inexpensive and provide you with almost instant silence. I'd recommend them when you find it impossible to study in a quiet place. But beware! Don't become so dependent on ear plugs that you can't study without them. Make an effort to seek out a quiet spot where you can study without ear plugs.

INTERNAL DISTRACTIONS

What do you mean by internal distractions?   Internal distractions, as the name implies, are ones which begin inside of your head. Below you'll find some advice for coping with these kinds of distractions.

Combating Internal Distractions

Plan ahead.
Don't daydream.
Deal with personal problems.
Deal with course anxiety.
Be realistic about your goals.
Use a reminder list.

How will planning ahead influence your concentration?   If you know what you're going to do next you won't have to think about it. It's the indecision which causes the distraction. If everything is planned in advance you can devote your full attention to the work at hand.

Halting Daydreams

Isn't it almost impossible to stop yourself from daydreaming? No. Although it may seem as though we slip into a daydream involuntarily, self-discipline can prevent this pitfall of concentration. Daydreaming may seem pleasant enough but it's really the mind's method for escaping work. Realizing this hard fact about daydreams should help you to deflect them.

Personal Problems

How do you deal with personal problems? If the problem is minor but nagging, your best bet is to write it down on a piece of paper and tell yourself that you will take care of it as soon as you've finished studying.

What if the problem is really serious? If the problem is really serious, there's no point in avoiding it. You must solve it or seek help in solving it, right away! Only then will you be able to concentrate fully.

Course Anxiety

Does it help to talk to the instructor if I feel anxious about a course? That's your best approach, If there's a course that's keeping you on edge go right to the instructor and lay your cards on the table. Often that will be all it takes to straighten out any problems you may have. If you're shy, you might prefer talking things over with a friend although that may not be as effective. One thing's for sure! It makes no sense to bottle up your anxiety. That can be damaging to your concentration and even to your overall health and well-being.

Setting Goals

How can you tell if your goals are realistic? If you haven't been studying much at all, it doesn't make sense to say "I'll study six hours every night." Chances are that it won't happen or if it does, you will burn yourself out for the rest of the week. A person who is out of shape doesn't start off by running a marathon. Goals must be achieved gradually.

Reminder Lists

Won't I remember things without using a reminder list? No. Forgetting happens massively and rapidly. In order to remember something without writing it down you would have to repeat it to yourself almost continuously. Obviously, that would destroy any concentration you had.

CONCENTRATION TIPS

Any other hints for improving concentration?   Yes. Here are a handful of proven tips and techniques that you may want to try.

TIPS AND TECHNIQUES FOR CONCENTRATION

1. **A positive attitude--**Hardly a tip. More like a way of life. If you tackle each assignment as an opportunity to learn instead of a task to complete, there's a far better chance that you will be able to maintain concentration.

2. **The spider technique--**A vibratiing tuning fork held close to a spider's web will send vibrations through the web itself. At first the spider will think that the motion is caused by a trapped insect. However, after a few more false alarms he soon learns to ignore the vibrations. You can use the same approach in the library every time the door opens. At first you'll be tempted to look up. But in time you'll learn to control the impulse and continue to concentrate.

3. **The no-room technique--**A form of self hypnosis, it works like this: Imagine that pathways of your mind are clogged with thoughts of the subject in front of you. As a result, there should be no room for any other thoughts.

4. **The checkmark technique--**Each time you find that you aren't concentrating, put a check on a blank sheet of paper. As you improve your concentration you'll discover that you make fewer and fewer checkmarks with each new assignment.

5. **The pencil technique--**This is one of the simplest, most effective ways to insure concentration. All you do is keep a pencil poised and ready whenever you are studying. If you're reading a textbook, for example, take time out every few paragraphs and jot down what the author has said so far. If you're at a loss for words then you should probably reread the portion that you didn't understand. The addition of a pencil should make a big difference. The fact that you are no longer reading passively will almost guarantee concentration.

FATIGUE

What about when you're just plain tired?   If you feel tired, you're going to have a tough time of concentrating. This physical fatigue can be brought about by deficiencies in diet, sleep or exercise.

Food

How does food affect fatigue?   Food provides you with energy and so it follows that if you don't have enough food or the right food that you are apt to be tired. One of the very best ways to combat fatigue is to start the day with a good breakfast.

What would you consider a good breakfast?   A good breakfast is made up of carbohydrates and protein. Although carbohydrates (things like donuts, danishes and juices) will provide you with energy, that energy will only be short-lived unless you add protein to your breakfast.

What does protein do?   Protein actually slows the rate at which the sugar from carbohydrates gets into your blood stream. Eat carbohydrates alone and your body will overreact, making you more tired than you were before breakfast. But add protein and that carbohydrate energy should sustain you 'til lunchtime and even beyond.

What foods are high in protein?   Meat and eggs are traditional high protein breakfast foods. However, you can get all the protein you really need (without the fat, cholesterol or cost) simply by adding two and one-half tablespoons of nonfat dry milk to a glass of whole or skim milk.

Sleep

How much sleep should I be getting?   Most doctors recommend that you get seven to nine hours of uninterrupted sleep each night. But the amount of sleep you get is only part of the picture.

What's the other part?   Equally important is a regular sleep cycle. If at all possible you should go to sleep at the same time every night. If your schedule varies too much your body won't know if it should be sleeping or waking.

Exercise

I really don't have time for exercises.   Everyone should have time for exercise. It serves as both a time saver and a life saver. A half hour of exercise each day should actually make you feel more alert when you sit down to study. As a result you will be thinking more clearly and efficiently than you would be if you hadn't exercised. Furthermore, doctors know that regular exercise can result in a longer, healthier more rewarding life.

"Mental Fatigue"

You've mentioned physical fatigue. Aren't there cases of mental fatigue?   Very rarely. Most of us use only a fraction of our mental energy. Normally what we think of as mental fatigue is really ordinary boredom.

Well then, how can I prevent boredom? There are a number of ways that you can prevent boredom. If you're studying, often all you need to do is to switch subjects for a while. However, if you find that one class consistently makes you sleepy, here's some advice you may want to follow.

FOUR WAYS TO BEAT BOREDOM

1. Try small group sessions--Instead of studying a subject by yourself all the time, make an effort to meet some of your classmates on a regular basis. Discussing a class with others may be all it takes to make the subject come alive. Furthermore, the enthusiasm that some group members have for the course is liable to be contagious.

2. Get individual tutoring--Nothing does a better job of robbing you of enthusiasm than failure. If you are having trouble with a course, don't just hang in there knowing less and less as everyone else is learning more and more. Get some help! A good tutor should put you back on track in a relatively short time.

3. Read alternative texts--Sometimes a textbook can be at the root of the problem. It may be that you are having trouble with the author's writing style instead of the class itself. If you and your textbook don't see eye to eye, try and find an alternative text which will explain things in a way that you'll understand. Then go back to your regular text and see if it doesn't make more sense to you now.

4. Use workbooks and programmed material--Some people can learn concepts by theory alone. But for many of us it takes real practice to make the ideas stick. Workbooks are an excellent way to put your textbook's ideas to work. Once you see the concepts in action there's a good chance that they'll make more sense to you.

MULTIPLE-CHOICE QUIZ

1. Concentration is
    a. distracting.
    b. thinking.
    c. unnecessary.
    d. effortless.

2. External distractions include
    a. sights.
    b. sounds.
    c. smells.
    d. all of the above.

3. The best spot for studying is probably
    a. your bedroom.
    b. a classroom.
    c. the library.
    d. a community center.

4. Good lighting must be
    a. high in contrast.
    b. low in glare.
    c. fluorescent.
    d. incandescent.

5. Many internal distractions can be eliminated by
    a. daydreaming.
    b. planning ahead.
    c. special earplugs.
    d. indecision.

6. Minor personal problems can be eased by
    a. writing them down.
    b. seeing a counselor.
    c. daydreaming.
    d. worrying.

7. The best way to remember something is to
    a. repeat it continuously.
    b. concentrate on it.
    c. write it down.
    d. make up a rhyme for it.

8. The "spider technique" is
    a. a method for ignoring distractions.
    b. a system for improving concentration.
    c. a technique that can be used in a library.
    d. all of the above.

9. One way to help combat fatigue is to
     a. eat plenty of sugary foods.
     b. drink a mixture of milk and dry milk.
     c. avoid eggs and other dairy products.
     d. have a small breakfast and a large lunch.

10. "Mental fatigue"
     a. is common and slightly dangerous.
     b. is usually a matter of boredom.
     c. can often be cured with a nap.
     d. none of the above.

3
YOUR MEMORY

FORGETTING

How big a problem is forgetting?

Gigantic. In fact, it's probably the greatest threat to your education. That's because forgetting happens massively and rapidly. Even if you read a textbook chapter carefully, you will forget most of it before the week is out. The same goes for listening to classroom lectures.

Is there anything I can do to stop this?

Above all, you have to *want* to remember. If that sounds silly, think about it. Many people downplay the power of forgetting and thus underestimate the importance of building their memory. No memory technique can help you to remember unless you are determined to do so.

But that's just an attitude. I want advice.

Once you have realized the value of remembering, the methods you can use are varied. What you choose many depend upon your personality. However, there is one method I strongly recommend for every student.

RECITATION

What method is that?

Recitation. By reciting what you've learned you

move information from your short-term memory where it is extremely vulnerable to forgetfulness to your long-term memory where it has a far better chance of sticking around.

So how does recitation work?

The idea of recitation is quite simple. Take what you have learned and repeat it out loud and in your own words.

How about an example?

Sure. Take a page from your notes. Put the information you have learned into categories, such as "Lincoln's personal life" or "The Lincoln-Douglas debates." Cover your note sheet except for the heading of your first category. Now recite the material in that category. When you finish take a look and see what you remembered and what you forgot.

You mean I'll still forget some of it?

Of course, but no instructor expects you to remember absolutely everything. Your goal should be to retain just the key ideas from your notes and textbook.

MORE MEMORY TECHNIQUES

What are some other memory techniques?

Distributed practice is one.

Sounds complicated.

Not really. All it involves is breakup your work into bite sized pieces. The brain is an amazing computer. But, like an electronic computer, it can malfunction if it gets overloaded with information. The solution? Take frequent study breaks. Marathon study sessions don't allow time for information to sink in. A ten minute break every hour will give your mind the consolidation time it needs to fasten facts into your memory.

Is there a better way to organize the information that I'm learning?

Yes, you can use the technique of categorization. When you cluster your information into groups or categories it suddenly becomes more manageable to recall. A classic example is the grocery list. If you try to remember a random list of items on the way to the store, there's a good chance that you will forget many of them.

Eggs	Tomatoes	Butter	Chicken
Beans	Ground Beef	Celery	Rice
Cereal	Carrots	Bacon	Bread
Spaghetti	Sausage	Milk	Yogurt

but if you put these foods into categories your chances of remembering will increase:

Meats	*Vegetables*	*Dairy*	*Grains*
Ground Beef	Beans	Eggs	Cereal
Sausage	Tomatoes	Butter	Spaghetti
Bacon	Carrots	Milk	Rice
Chicken	Celery	Yogurt	Bread

How about some other memory techniques?

Here are two more widely accepted memory methods.

Two More Memory Methods

Mental Visualization--The more of your mind you use the safer a piece of information will be from forgetting. That's why it is an excellent idea to draw pictures of some of the things you learn. You don't need to be Da Vinci. Stick figures will do. For example, if you learn that Martin Van Buren was the first native-born American President (born in New York in 1782), you can easily turn that fact into a picture. Try it! [See Figure 3.1]

The Link--You say you keep forgetting that Fulton invented the Steamboat? Just think of a **full ton** (perhaps you imagine a big black weight with one ton written on it) weighing down a **steamboat,** causing it to sink. With a little imagination, inventors and their inventions, scientists and their discoveries, almost anything, can be linked together with an outrageous picture. If the picture is vivid, your memory will be too. [See Figure 3.2]

Figure 3.1 Mental Visualization.   You don't have to be an artist in order to illustrate a fact with a picture.

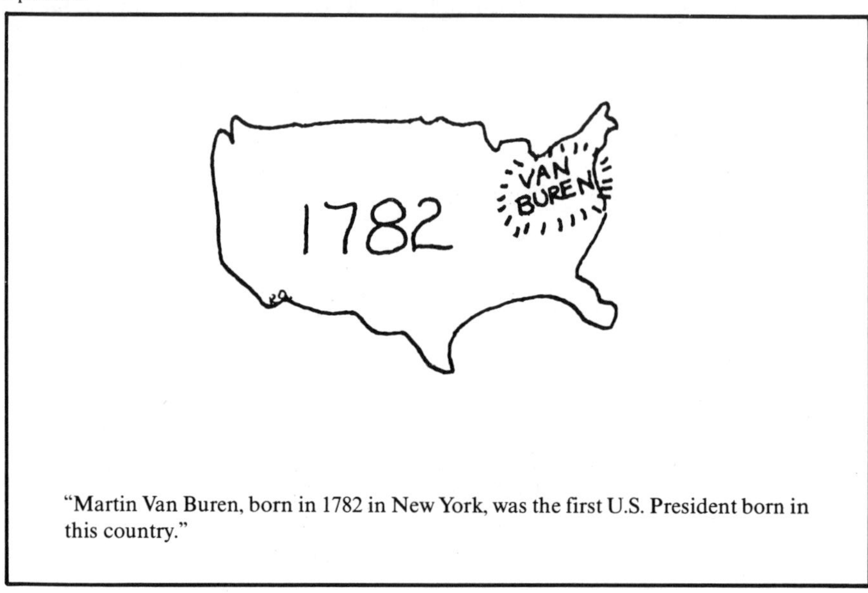

"Martin Van Buren, born in 1782 in New York, was the first U.S. President born in this country."

Figure 3.2   The Link, *New* information can be remembered more easily when it is imaginatively linked up with *old* information.

MNEMONIC DEVICES

What about tricks like "thirty days have September" and "i before e"?

Those "tricks" are known as mnemonics and unfortunately there are only a limited number of ready-made mnemonics available. The solution is, of course, to make your own mnemonics.

How do I do that?

One way is to make a word. People who have an interest in music know that FACE is a great way to remember the notes in the spaces of the treble clef (F, A, C and E). You can use the same method for other facts that you want to remember.

The Make-A-Word-Mnemonic

The FOIL method for the multiplication of two binomials is a common example of a make-a-word mnemonic. The procedure for constructing such a mnemonic, is simple:

1. Take the information you want to remember and underline a key word in each main point or step:

   a. multiply the *first* number in each expression.
   b. multiply the *outer* numbers.
   c. multiply the *inner* numbers.
   d. multiply the *last* number in each expression.

2. Take the first letter from each key word: F, O, I, L.

3. Construct a word from these letters: FOIL

Yes, but not all things can be made into words.

That's true. If you're having a tough time constructing a make-a-word mnemonic, I have several suggestions: 1) Find a synonym for one of the key words which begins with a "better letter." 2) Pick out a different word in the step or point which will remind you of the key word. 3) If the order of your facts isn't important, try rearranging them to see if they will form a word.

What if none of these suggestions work?

You could try a make-a-sentence mnemonic. Imagine the frustration of the music teacher who found that the notes which rest on the lines of the treble clef (E, G, B, D and F) wouldn't spell out a word as easily as the notes on the spaces (F, A, C and E) did. Obviously he couldn't pick a synonym for any of the notes. Nor could he rearrange their order. But when he used these notes to make a sentence, he hit paydirt. Music students still learn the sentence "Every Good Boy Does Fine," probably the best known of the make-a-sentence mnemonics.

The Make-A-Sentence Mnemonic

Let's pretend that you couldn't come up with a make-a-word mnemonic for multiplying binomials.

1. Underline a key word in each main point or step.
2. Write down the letters from the key words: F, O, I, L.
3. Construct a sentence that is easy to remember, using words whose first letters are the same as the first letters of the key words:

> _F_iguring _o_bviously _i_nvolves _l_ogic.

MULTIPLE-CHOICE QUIZ

1. Forgetting is
     a. the greatest threat to your education.
     b. a problem but not a serious one.
     c. easily defeated with careful re-reading.
     d. a problem that only affects reading.

2. In order to combat forgetting successfully, you must first
     a. take commercial memory courses.
     b. use key words and abbreviations.
     c. have an interest in remembering.
     d. none of the above.

3. Recitation combats forgetting by
     a. moving information to your long-term memory.
     b. moving information to your short-term memory.
     c. placing information into categories.
     d. adding interest to the memory process.

4. Reciting should be done
    a. silently and in your own words.
    b. silently and verbatim.
    c. out loud and in your own words.
    d. out loud and verbatim.

5. Effective reading should enable you to remember
    a. all key ideas.
    b. all supporting details.
    c. all examples.
    d. all of the above.

6. The idea behind distributed practice is to
    a. study for as long as possible.
    b. break up your studying into small parts.
    c. rest for an hour in the middle of the evening.
    d. prevent your memory from consolidating.

7. Categorization is effective
    a. because it clusters information.
    b. because it forces recitation.
    c. only if you use four categories.
    d. only when remembering grocery lists.

8. Mental visualization requires
    a. no real artistic ability.
    b. using more of your mind.
    c. transforming thoughts into pictures.
    d. all of the above.

9. Memory tricks are known as
    a. pneumatics.
    b. mnemonics.
    c. mimetics.
    d. syllogics.

10. Key information can be remembered when it is converted into a
    a. sentence.
    b. word.
    c. rhyme.
    d. all of the above.

4
THE CORNELL
NOTETAKING SYSTEM

THE NECESSITY OF NOTETAKING

Is notetaking really necessary? If you want to remember what you've read or heard, then notetaking is a necessity. It gives you a fighting chance against that arch villain, forgetting.

Is forgetting that much of a problem? You bet! One expert estimates that you forget about 80% of a textbook chapter or classroom lecture just two weeks after you've read or heard it.

But doesn't notetaking get in the way? No! Notetaking won't interfere with your ability to listen or read. In fact, it should help to make you more awake and alert.

NOTETAKING GUIDELINES

How do I begin taking notes? You can start by using telegraphic sentences. Your purpose when taking notes is not to transcribe a lecture or recopy a textbook. What you want is a streamlined version of the lecture or textbook chapter. Telegraphic sentences help you reach this goal by reducing important sentences down to their key elements. [See Figure 4.1]

Figure 4.1   Telegraphic Sentence Illustrated

Lecturer's actual words

At Gettysburg was fought the most decisive battle of the War Between the States, marking the turning point of the struggle between North and South.

Student's telegraphic sentence

Gettysburg = MOST DECISIVE BATTLE - - TURNING POINT!

What information should I be including in my notes?   First, you'll be looking for the main ideas and sub-ideas. You will also want to copy down any important examples and details.

Should I recopy my notes after I get home?   No. It makes no sense to recopy your notes. That can waste great amounts of time. What does make sense is to take legible notes in the first place, and thus eliminate the need to recopy.

Modified
Printing

Should my notes be printed or written?   Neither. Printing takes time and cursive writing is apt to be difficult to read. The solution is a compromise known as the modified printing style, diagrammed in Figure 4.2. It provides the speed of cursive with the neatness of printing and, as you can see from the illustration, it is easy to learn.

Figure 4.2   The Modified Printing Style Illustrated

The modified printing style is really a double time saver: first it's fast; and second, it should eliminate completely the time-consuming chore of recopying your notes. Try it! It's easy to learn and faster than you think.

Wouldn't shorthand be an even better solution?   No. For two reasons. First of all, not everyone knows shorthand and it takes a considerable amount of time to learn. Second, shorthand must be transcribed soon after it has been written. That takes time, the kind of time that most students simply don't have.

Do you have any other advice for taking notes?   Yes. Here are six rules designed to improve your notetaking.

Six Rules for Better Notetaking

1. **Keep notes in one place**--Have a separate notebook for the notes of each subject.

2. **Use standard size paper**--Don't cheat yourself on needed space.

3. **Leave blanks in your notes**--If there's something that you didn't catch or understand, leave a space and then get a friend or the instructor to help you fill it in later.

4. **Use a system for numbering or indenting**--A number of them are suggested in this chapter. Or, make up your own.

5. **Devise abbreviations for words that you use often**--This should speed up the notetaking process.

6. **Separate your thoughts**--If something occurs to you while you're taking notes, by all means, write it down. But put it in brackets so you know it's your own idea.

THE CORNELL SYSTEM

What is the Cornell System? The Cornell System is a method for notetaking that was developed more than thirty years ago at Cornell University. It remains one of the most effective systems ever devised.

The Cue
Column

How does the Cornell System work? The secret of the Cornell System is the cue column, a two and-one-half inch margin at the lefthand side of each notebook page. It can be drawn in fairly easily with a ruler and a pen. In addition, some companies now manufacture paper which already comes with this special margin. [See Figure 4.3].

Won't a standard margin do just as well? No. The traditional one and one-quarter inch margin isn't wide enough for our purposes.

Is it okay to use a spiral notebook? Another no. In order for the system to work properly, you should use loose-leaf paper. That way you will be able to remove and replace note sheets whenever you want.

Figure 4.3   The Cornell Notetaking System Diagramed and Explained

<table>
<tr><td>----------------2½----------------</td><td>----------------6----------------</td></tr>
<tr><td>

Reduce ideas and facts
to concise jottings and
summaries as cues
for **Reciting,
Reviewing,** and
Reflecting.

(CUE COLUMN)
</td><td>

Record the lecture as fully
and as meaningfully as possible.

(NOTETAKING COLUMN)
</td></tr>
</table>

THE CORNELL NOTETAKING SYSTEM

1. **Record.**   In the Notetaking Column, record as many meaningful facts and ideas as you can. Use telegraphic sentences; but, make sure you will be able to gain full meaning later. Write legibly.

2. **Reduce.**   After class, summarize your notes by writing in single words and short phrases in the Cue Column. Summarizing clarifies meanings, reveals relationships, establishes continuity, and strengthens memory. Also, this thinking and writing of cues sets up a perfect stage for studying for exams later.

3. **Recite.**   Cover the Notetaking Column with a sheet of paper. Then, looking at the words and phrases in the Cue Column only, recite aloud and in your own words the full lecture.

4. **Reflect.**   Professor Hans Bethe, nuclear physicist and Nobel Prize winner, said, "...creativity comes only through reflection." You reflect by asking yourself the following questions, for example, What's the significance of these facts? What principle are they based on? How can I apply them? How do they fit in with what I already know? What's beyond them?

5. **Review.**   Spend ten minutes every week reviewing your notes. If you do so, you'll retain a great deal for current use, as well as, for the exam, which comes later.

Summary.   Leave space at the bottom of each sheet for a summary.

What is the cue column designed for?   Notes will be recorded in the large righthand side column of each note sheet. Then later on, key words and phrases will be written in the cue column in order to guarantee that these important ideas are not forgotten. More details on the use of the cue column will be covered in Chapter 6.

Notetaking
Formats   *Should I take my notes in outline form?*   No. Outlines are a bad idea when it comes to taking notes.

Why?   The format of an outline is so restrictive that you are apt to pay more attention to the letters and Roman numerals that you are to the lecture or textbook chapter.

Well then, what should my notes look like?   There are several different formats that you can use, depending upon the type of lecture you are attending or textbook you are reading.

Notetaking Formats

Definition--Made up entirely of brief definitions or explanations of words and terms.

Sentence--Good for notes which don't fit the definition format. Best for notes which emphasize ideas and concepts. Remember to make the sentences telegraphic.

Topic and idea--Excellent for lectures where the speaker mentions an idea and then expands upon it or in textbooks which contain a lot of subheadings. Use topics as headings and put supporting materials beneath them.

Paragraph--Look like paragraphs but aren't. The main purpose is to avoid the outline format. Make all sentences brief.

Summaries

How do you feel about summaries?   Summaries are a great idea! They give your first chance to show what you have learned. Writing a summary is almost like taking your own quiz. You know right away if you've understood what you've been taking notes on.

How do I fit a summary into my notes?   There are three ways you can do it: 1) You can summarize each page of notes, 2) you can summarize the entire lecture or textbook chapter or 3) you can do both. In each case, the summary space is made by drawing a horizontal line about two inches from the bottom of the page.

Which summary method do you recommend?   The third option summarizing each page as well as the entire lecture or chapter takes the most time and effort, but I am convinced that it yields the greatest rewards. When it comes time to review your notes you'll be able to see page by page how you arrived at your final summary. Furthermore, each summary you write will give you the kind of practice you'll need to prepare for demanding exam questions.

Do you have an example that illustrates the Cornell System? Yes. Here's one that I usually use in the classroom. Notice that this example shows the three sections: the wide note-taking column, the cue column, and the summary. [See Figure 4.4].

Figure 4.4   Using Words and Phrases in Cue Column Illustrated

	Biology 101 – Prof. Fairbanks – Sept 18th ①
Water affects weight – helps metabolize fat	A. Importance of water in controlling weight 　1. Water helps body metabolize stored fat. 　2. Studies show:
Increase water = 　decrease fat	a. Increase water intake = fat deposits decrease 　　b. Decrease " " = " " increase
Decrease water = 　increase fat	3. Why? Kidneys can't function at capacity w/o 　　enough water; so, some of the kidney's work 　　is dumped on liver.
Kidney – liver 　relationship	a. Liver's job is to metabolize fat. 　　b. If liver does kidney's work, too; can't complete 　　　its own work. 　　c. So, liver metabolizes less fat, thus more fat 　　　is stored.
water affects hunger	d. If there's sufficient water; then, liver & 　　　kidneys do their complete jobs. Furthermore, 　　　this leads to a natural loss of hunger, which 　　　means the intake of fewer calories.
Daily = 2 qts	4. How much water? 　　a. 2 qts. every day = 8 large glasses (8 oz.)
Overweight = 1 extra glass per 25 lbs.	b. If overweight = one additional glass for 　　　every 25 lbs. of excess weight.

Water keeps body's fluids in perfect balance. Water enables kidneys to function at maximum level; thus, freeing liver to metabolize (burn) stored fat. To achieve weight loss, drink 8 glasses (8 oz. ones) of water. More, if already overweight.

Did you use the formal outline method? No. It looks as if I did; but, the letters and numbers merely separate the various points made by the lecturer.

How did you arrive at the words and phrases in the cue column? Well, I put words that I could associate with the points made by the lecturer. Of course, these words and phrases could differ slightly from student to student.

How did you make up the summary? This took some thinking and re-reading of the notes to come up with a hard-hitting, straightforward statement -- one that I would write on an exam. Again, the wording could differ from student to student.

Are there other systems?   Aside from just personal, home-made systems, I know of none. I do, however, have a system that is based on the Cornell System; but, with an important variation in the way you use the cue column. [See Figure 4.5].

What's the variation?   Instead of writing just words and phrases, you write actual questions based on the notes.

Figure 4.5   Using the Question-Technique in the Cue Column Illustrated

What are some signs of sleep loss?	Psychology 102 – Prof. William James – October 14th
	A. Chronic sleep loss in college students
	1. Problem: feel drowsy, fatigued, weary = suffering sleep loss.
	Ex. find lectures, mind wanders, none or poor notes, poor concentration, irritable, no enthusiasm, always feel sleepy.
What's the objective of sleep?	2. Objective of sleep = to promote daytime alertness.
How many hours are needed by ages 4-14?	3. Facts from Sleep Disorder Center at Stanford University:
	a. Ages 4 to 14 = need 9-10 hrs. sleep.
How many hours needed by age 15+?	b. Ages 15 & older = still need 9-10 hrs. sleep at night.
	c. Tests show: only 8 hrs. sleep = daytime alertness impaired.
Is sleep loss cumulative?	d. Sleep loss is cumulative: lose 1 hr. per night, by Friday sleeploss is almost pathological. Performance impaired.
What's the biological clock?	4. Your biological clock
When is sleep the best?	a. When your sleepy period coincides with bedtime, your sleep will be longest & deepest. Then, your daytime activities will be most zestful & energetic.
What are the usual results of optimum sleep?	b. With sufficient sleep, you won't be sleepy after lunch, nor fall asleep in class. You'll be able to concentrate & work.
Who's the director of the Sleep Disorder Center?	5. What to do? Dr. William Dement, director of Sleep Disorder Center at Stanford School of Medicine recommends:
What's a good sleep environment?	a. Create good environment. A quiet, dark, secure room. Use only for sleeping.
What's the single most important rule?	b. Regularity. Adhere strictly to same hours. Single most important rule!
How can you achieve synchrony?	c. Achieve Synchrony. By maintaining regularity, your biological clock & rhythm will shift to accomodate your schedule.
What's the recommended length of sleep?	d. Length. Sleep 9½ hours on a regular basis.
What other routines are recommended?	e. Daily Routine. Exercise daily, eat at same time, good diet.
How about drugs?	f. Drugs. Alcohol, sleeping pills, caffeine, amphetamines damage sleep-mechanism.
Does optimum sleep add years to your life?	6. Optimum sleep promotes not only a more alert, energetic, zestful life; but also, a longer life according to some studies.
How long were puppies kept awake?	7. Sleep revitalizes body
What happened?	Experiment: Puppies kept awake 4-6 days died – never waking after permitted to fall asleep.

Most college students experience chronic sleep loss. The evidence is their feeling drowsy & fatigued continually, falling asleep in class, finding it hard to concentrate, and irritableness. Dr. Dement's findings show that college students need between 9-10 hours of sleep. He strongly recommends getting in synchrony with one's biological clock by sleeping in a quiet, dark room, at regular hours, about 9½ hours nightly; also, by exercising daily, eating good food habitually, and avoiding drugs, alcohol, & caffeine.

A final kicker: optimum sleep promotes a longer life.

Which is the better system?   Well, both systems are effective. Some students like to recite from the cues provided by words and phrases, while others prefer to recite by answering questions. Incidentally, those using the question-technique report enthusiastically that they often find the same or similar questions on their exams.

When should you write the cue words or the questions?   The sooner the better! If you have a free period directly after the lecture, do it then before forgetting takes its toll. At the latest, fill in the cue column during your study time in the same evening.

MULTIPLE-CHOICE QUIZ

1. Notetaking is chiefly designed to combat
    a. boredom.
    b. memory.
    c. listening.
    d. forgetting.

2. In lecture notetaking, your sentences should be
    a. telegraphic.
    b. recopied.
    c. increased.
    d. transcribed.

3. A good set of notes should include
    a. main ideas.
    b. sub-ideas.
    c. important examples and details.
    d. all of the above.

4. Notes should be
    a. printed.
    b. typed.
    c. written in cursive.
    d. written in modified printing.

5. Shorthand for notetaking is
    a. easy to learn and transcribe.
    b. risky and impractical.
    c. a time-saving technique.
    d. increasingly popular.

6. Thoughts you may have about a subject should be
    a. blended in with the rest of your notes.
    b. saved until after class.
    c. separated with brackets.
    d. written in a different notebook.

7. The real secret of the Cornell System is
    a. the cue column.
    b. the spiral notebook.
    c. a standard margin.
    d. a ruler.

8. In the Cornell System, notes are taken
    a. on the entire page.
    b. on the right side of the page.
    c. in lefthand margin.
    d. in the summary area.

9. One format that is *not* recommended for Cornell notetaking is
    a. definition.
    b. paragraph.
    c. outline.
    d. topic and idea.

10. Summaries are
    a. your first chance to show what you know.
    b. almost like taking your very own quiz.
    c. helpful when put at the bottom of each page.
    d. all of the above.

5
CLASSROOM LECTURES

How can I get the most out of a classroom lecture?

By listening carefully and taking complete notes.

LISTENING

Isn't just plain listening good enough?

You will not be able to retain the ideas of a lecture simply by listening.

Even if my hearing is good?

Even so. You see, listening to a lecture isn't simply a matter of hearing it. To listen properly you must take the words that you hear and convert them into ideas. These ideas must then be moved from your short term memory to your long term memory so they have a better chance of lasting.

How many of the ideas will be forgotten?

As we mentioned in the last chapter, all but 20% of a lecture will fade from memory within two weeks. The shocking fact is that over 50% of a lecture is forgotten almost immediately.

How can I become a better listener?

Good listening is a matter of three essential skills:

Triple-A Listening

1. ATTITUDE--You must walk into the lecture with a good attitude. Don't assume the subject is going to be dull or that the speaker is going to be wrong. If you do disagree with something, write it down instead of stewing about it. Above all, give the speaker the benefit of the doubt, at least while the lecture is going on.

2. ATTENTION--You won't learn much if you don't pay attention. Some students simply fake attention and then drift off into a daydream. Others are easily bothered by external distractions. In order to profit from a lecture you must pay attention and maintain that attention.

3. ADJUSTMENT--Listening is an activity that involves constant adjustment. Good listeners don't listen to a lecture simply for the facts. They want to know how these facts are tied together. As a result, they build a framework of the facts that they hear. More importantly, they adjust this framework, if necessary, when new facts are introduced.

TAKING NOTES

What is the point of taking lecture notes?

Lecture notes are used to capture the lecturer's ideas on paper so you can take this information home and study it.

How do I begin my lecture notetaking?

With anticipation. You must gear up for the notetaking which lies ahead. Do this by getting to class a little early or at least on time. Then find a seat where you can see and hear everything that the lecturer does and says. Then, when the lecture begins, you begin, by taking thoughtful and complete notes.

What sort of things should I be writing down?

You'll want to keep a record of all the main ideas as well as the supporting details. In general, your goal is to emerge from the classroom with enough notes to form a full-bodied concept.

How can I tell the main idea from the rest?

Most speakers drop pretty good clues around the main ideas of their lecture. One of the most common signals is a change of voice. The speaker's voice may suddenly become louder, softer, or slower and more precise. Other clues include one sentence summaries which often follow a main idea and transistional words which frequently pave the way from one main idea to the next.

Should I take notes on ideas that sound ordinary?

Yes. You may not realize how important an ordinary-sounding idea really is until later. Of course, if the idea turns out to be as ordinary as it sounded, there is nothing that says you have to study it.

Should I take my notes in my own words?

No. Although it is important for you to "translate" what you've learned into your own words, that can come later. During the lecture your number one priority is to get everything important on paper. The best way to do this is by using telegraphic sentences.

What if the lecturer speaks too quickly?

If you are unable to keep up, even with telegraphic sentences, then I would suggest that you go with the two-page notetaking system.

The Two-Page Notetaking System

Open your notebook out or put two blank sheets of note paper side by side.
   ON THE LEFT PAGE:
      record only the lecturer's main ideas.
   ON THE RIGHT PAGE:
      write down the details across from the main ideas that they pertain to.
You'll end up with the lecture's most important information, in brief, on the left, as well as the supporting details on the right.

How do you feel about abbreviations?

Abbreviations in notetaking are a fine idea as long as you don't abuse them. The best bet is to add abbreviations gradually to your notetaking routine. If you inject too many at once you may not be able to read your own notes.

Any other advice on lecture notetaking?

Here are seven rules that you'll want to adopt.

Seven Rules for Lecture Notetaking

1. Put the name and number of the course, the date and the lecturer's name at the top of the first sheet for each lecture. This will avoid any mix-ups and should make reviewing a lot easier.

2. Don't doodle, knit or do any activity other than notetaking during a lecture. You are apt to interfere with concentration, both yours and the lecturer's.

3. Don't just take notes passively. Be academically aggressive. Work hard to concentrate and extract everything valuable out of a lecture.

4. Be alert for clues. Signal words like *so, therefore, first,* and *finally* may tip you off as to the lecturer's organizational pattern. Other phrases like "This is a common pitfall" or "You'll see this later" will help you to decide what facts should be emphasized in your notes.

5. Use a symbol (an asterisk, arrow, etc) to mark ideas the lecturer emphasizes.

6. Record the lecturer's examples. They will often clarify abstract ideas. Use a special notation (like Ex) to indicate that they are examples.

7. Pay as close attention to the end of the lecture as to the beginning. Many students miss the beginning of the lecture because they are still turning pages, finding pens, or settling down. By the same token, many students miss the end of a lecture because they are already preparing to move on to the next class. And yet, the beginning and end of the lecture are often the most important. The beginning will frequently include a summary or an explanation that will make the rest of the lecture more understandable. The end not only contains important conclusions, but will often be highly concentrated if the lecturer realizes that time is short and that half of the content must be squeezed in, in just a few minutes.

LECTURE ODDS AND ENDS

Wouldn't it make sense to tape the lecture instead of taking notes?

No. Taping the lecture will wind up doing you more harm than good. To begin with, if the recorder is running, there's less incentive to listen to the lecture. As a result, any questions you may have will probably only occur to you after you're home. Secondly, you'll still have to take notes in order to remember the key points from the lecture. That means devoting a lot of time to transcribing the tape, time that you could have been using for study.

Is there a way to walk into a lecture better prepared?

One simple, but highly effective way to prepare for the day's lecture is to go over your notes from the previous lecture. This way the stage will be set when you enter the classroom. You'll know just where the speaker left off.

Is it okay to miss a lecture or two?

Not if you can help it. Don't be fooled by the idea that you can skip a lecture and simply copy someone's notes. A lot of crucial information is almost certain to be lost in the translation. Furthermore, by skipping the lecture you are cheating yourself out of the chance to ask questions of the speaker, as they occur to you. There is nothing more tragic than a student whose failure in a course hinges on a single question that was left unasked and unanswered.

What if I can't help missing a lecture?

I realize that there may be circumstances beyond control that will cause you to miss a lecture. If you know that you'll be missing a class or two, my advice is to make a friend who will serve as a reliable contact for those times.

TV COURSES

What are TV courses?

Many community and junior colleges have arrangements with local public or cable TV stations to broadcast college lectures for those students who are unable, or simply choose not to attend regular courses at their community or junior college.

Do I have to go to the college at all if I take a TV course?

Yes, although registration for these courses can often be done through the mail or by phone, you must show up at the college for the final exam and often, for a midterm as well. In addition, some instructors may schedule additional meetings for class discussions.

How should I take notes for TV lectures?

Take them as you would for any lecture course, paying close attention to the instructor's main ideas.

Are TV lectures easier than classroom lectures?

TV lectures are clearly more convenient than classroom lectures. However, they are seldom easier. Simply because they are being broadcast on TV does not mean that they have been simplified for a general audience. If anything, TV lectures are harder, because they require an extra dose of self-discipline.

Any advice for improving my self-discipline in a TV course?

Yes. Here are a number of suggestions that are especially designed for watching a TV lecture.

Watching a TV Lecture

1. Have your set tuned and ready several minutes before the lecture is ready to begin. Make an effort not to watch any conventional television shows immediately before or after the lecture.

2. Do not eat or talk during the lecture.

3. Ask friends and family not to call you during the time that the lecture will be telecast. Or better yet, unhook your telephone.

4. Keep your hands free for notetaking. Don't iron, fold laundry or do other household chores during the lecture.

5. Watch the lecture from a sitting position. Do not lie down on a bed or couch.

6. Try to sit in a chair that you do not normally use for watching TV. The change of chairs may have the psychological effect of convincing you that the lecture is serious business, not just prime time entertainment.

7. If you share your home with a person or pet, make arrangements not to be interrupted during the lecture.

8. Keep potential distractions out of reach and out of sight until the lecture is over.

I have a videocassette recorder (VCR). Is it okay if I tape the lectures?

Although taping the lecture may sound convenient, I wouldn't recommend it. In a course that is so dependent upon your self-discipline, a video machine could be your undoing. Here's why:

Why You Shouldn't Videotape Your TV Lecture

1. *Taping hurts your notetaking.* The knowledge that you are taping the lecture may discourage you from taking complete notes. If you take only minimal notes with the idea that you will view the videotaped lecture again later on, you may be creating trouble for yourself. The chances that you will watch the lecture a second time are slim.

2. *Taping the lecture is no substitute for notetaking.* If you have chosen to tape the lecture *instead* of taking notes, you are making the same mistake as the student who records a classroom lecture on audio tape. This is one of the most inefficient ways in which to learn your material. In the time it takes to watch the lecture for a second time you probably could have reviewed the key ideas from several lectures, preserved in a far more manageable form, in your notebook.

3. *You'll never find a "more convenient time."* If you plan to tape the lecture so you can view it at a more convenient time, perhaps you shouldn't be taking the lecture at all. If you don't make time right away, you may wind up with a stack of unwatched lectures at the end of the semester.

MULTIPLE-CHOICE QUIZ

1. The best way to retain a classroom lecture is
   a. listen carefully without taking notes.
   b. concentrate on getting everything on paper.
   c. listen and take notes.
   d. use a cassette recorder.

2. After two weeks all that you'll remember from a lecture is about
   a. 20% of it.
   b. 40% of it.
   c. 60% of it.
   d. 80% of it.

3. Listening is an activity that involves
   a. constant adjustment.
   b. genuine attention.
   c. a positive attitude.
   d. all of the above.

4. Your goal is to emerge from the lecture with
    a. a sense of anticipation.
    b. a full-bodied concept.
    c. supporting details.
    d. none of the above.

5. One of the clues which does *not* signal a main idea is a
    a. change in the speaker's tone of voice.
    b. sentence that begins with "For instance."
    c. one sentence summary.
    d. transitional word or phrase.

6. If the lecturer speaks too quickly, you should try using
    a. full sentences.
    b. the spider technique.
    c. the 2-page notetaking system.
    d. a cue column.

7. Abbreviations in your notetaking should be
    a. added gradually.
    b. avoided entirely.
    c. used almost exclusively.
    d. approved by the instructor.

8. One simple but highly effective way to prepare for a lecture is to
    a. meet with the instructor before class.
    b. copy someone else's lecture notes.
    c. read over your textbook's introduction.
    d. go over your notes from the previous lecture.

9. Compared to classroom lectures, TV lectures are usually
    a. shorter.
    b. easier.
    c. more convenient.
    d. all of the above.

10. "Attending" a TV lecture often requires more
    a. distractions.
    b. self-discipline.
    c. notebook paper.
    d. registration.

6
TEXTBOOK ASSIGNMENTS

PREPARATION

What's the best way to tackle a textbook assignment? The very best way to tackle all of your textbook assignments is to start working on them even before the semester begins.

But I won't know my assignments until after the semester begins. Yes, but you should know what textbooks you'll be using. Check the list and buy your books ahead of schedule. Then, flip through each book in order to become acquainted with it. Read the chapter titles and glance at things such as headings, subheadings and even picture captions. Finally, take a few moments to read the preface and the introduction.

The
Preface
What good will it do to read the preface? Far too many students think of the preface as a boring page that can be easily skipped. On the contrary, the preface gives you a rare and exciting opportunity to see the author drop his scholarly style and write like a "regular person".

What will the preface tell me that I can't find elsewhere in the book? Here are five things which you should find in almost any preface.

What's in a Preface?

1. **What the author's objective is**--why is he or she writing the book.

2. **What the author's objective is not**--Says "if you're looking for this, you won't find it here."

3. **The way the book is organized**--The preface can often provide you with a road map for the entire book.

4. **How and why the book is different**--Here's your chance to find out what's new, what this book has to offer.

5. **The author's qualifications**--You wouldn't read a book on auto mechanics written by a biologist, and vice versa. This is where the author spells out the qualifications which make him or her an expert.

The Intro-
duction

How does the introduction differ from the preface?   Where the preface tends to be broad and general in its scope, the introduction is just the opposite: narrow and specific.

Give me one good reason why I should read the introduction.   I'll give you four instead.

FOUR REASONS FOR READING THE INTRODUCTION

REASON #1:   It's well-written. Although many people judge a book by its cover, others go by the introduction instead.

REASON #2:   It's highly concentrated. Because its space is limited, the introduction is usually packed with facts.

REASON #3:   It's a stage-setter. The rest of the book is easier to understand once you've read the introduction.

REASON #4:   It's a daily warm-up. Add underlinings and marginal notes so you can review the introduction again and again as a way of preparing for each day's assignment.

SURVEYING

Is there anything else I can do to warm up once the semester has begun?   You can take the same approach that you took for the entire textbook, but on a smaller scale. Before you begin reading each chapter, gear up for it by taking time out for a quick survey.

How can surveying help me? Surveying creates an instant background. When the time comes to read the chapter you will already be familiar with many of its ideas and terms. In short, There should be no surprises. As a result, you will approach the chapter with understanding and confidence. Furthermore, the chapter's headings and subheadings can then be used as advance organizers.

What are advance organizers? Advance organizers are magnetic centers which draw the facts and ideas of a textbook like iron filings. Without them, you have only a scattering of facts. As magnetic centers, the headings and subheadings will draw these facts together and organize them effectively.

READING YOUR TEXTBOOK

What is the most thorough way to go about reading a textbook chapter? Read each book as it was written: paragraph by paragraph. At the end of every paragraph, ask yourself the same question: What did the author just say? If you can answer that question, it's safe to read on. If not, then you should probably re-read the troublesome paragraph.

Is there any other way that I can be sure that the paragraph-by-paragraph method is working effectively? Yes. You can quiz yourself on the content of the chapter by turning the headings and sub-headings into questions. If you are unable to answer these questions, then the chances are good that you have failed to extract the important information from the chapter.

Isn't there a well-known reading method which uses this procedure? Yes. The SQ3R reading method was developed by Francis Robinson in 1941. The Q stands for Questions and calls for essentially the same procedure that we have just discussed. Although I wholeheartedly endorse the steps used in the SQ3R, I think it is lacking one crucial step: Reflection.

Reflection provides creatively. It simply involves taking what you've read and giving it some extra thought in order to explore its implications and further uses. I've taken that reflection step and added it to the SQ3R method to make what I think is an unbeatable reading system. Here are the steps for the New SQ4R method:

THE SQ4R SYSTEM

S   SURVEY — Surveying overcomes procrastination. It gets you started.

Q   QUESTION — Turn each heading into a question and notice how it focuses your attention.

R1 READ — With a goal of answering your question, reading with concentration should come naturally.

R2 RECORD — Write down brief notes of ideas, facts or details from the reading. These will serve as cues in future review sessions.

R3 RECITE — Reciting aloud means thinking and thinking is the only way to make memories stick. Cover your page so that only your marginal notes can be seen. Use these notes as cues and recite out loud and in your own words, the ideas, facts and details that you've covered.

R4 REFLECT — Reflection helps to weave new ideas into old, by comparing those new ideas with ones you already know. By asking yourself, "What are these ideas and facts based on?" and "How can I use them?" you should increase your creativity, your knowledge and even your I.Q!

Asking Questions

What if I read something over and over and still can't understand it? The first impulse is to turn to a friend or instructor right away and say "I don't understand this." However, you will aid both yourself and your helper by taking some time to determine exactly what you don't understand. By carefully defining your problem you should have a clearer idea of the solution. In fact, many students who take this approach wind up answering their own questions!

TAKING TEXTBOOK NOTES

Now that I know how to read my textbook, how do I go about taking notes? Take notes after every paragraph, either in your text or separately. If you are using the paragraph-by-paragraph reading method, either procedure should fit in quite easily. Both methods have their advantages and disadvantages.

What are the advantages and disadvantages of marking your textbook? The chief advantage of marking your textbook is convenience. Your textbook and your notebook become one and the same. Important ideas and facts can be underlined or circled with ease. The primary disadvantage of marking your textbook is, of course, that you are putting marks on your textbook that cannot be easily erased. Students who mark their textbooks often find that marks they once made early in the semester are no longer important later on. As a result, this de-emphasizes those markings which are truly important.

Do you approve of using a highlighter? Although highlighters come in every shape and color, a sharp pencil gives you far more versatility than any of them. With a pencil you can circle key words, number and letter items and write in marginal notes. A marker is too thick for such fine work. Furthermore, in a pinch, your pencil marks can be erased. No such luck with a highlighter.

How long should my marginal notes be? Long enough to cover the subject, but short enough to promote genuine thinking. If the notes are too long, there'll be nothing to learn. If the notes are too brief, you won't have enough information to remember the facts or ideas that are called for.

What are the pros and cons of taking separate notes? Without a doubt, separate notetaking promotes more active thinking. After all, you won't be circling or underlining key facts. You'll be writing them out. Furthermore, when it comes time for review, your separate notes can serve as an alternate textbook. You'll be able to put your real textbook aside and study from a few sheets of paper instead. As for the disadvantages of taking separate notes, the main drawback is that it takes more time. However, time spent early in the semester may be time saved during exam week when each minute is precious.

What guidelines can you suggest for marking a textbook or taking separate notes? Figure 6.1 provides a fast reference guide for both procedures.

How am I supposed to deal with outside readings? Outside readings are a special case. They should not be studied as carefully as your primary text but they should not be ignored. Here are some suggestions on how to approach them.

Figure 6.1   Some Guidelines for **MARKING YOUR TEXTBOOK OR TAKING NOTES**

	Marking your textbook	Taking notes
The System	Use lines and circles for marking or make up your own system. Whatever method you choose, be consistent!	Use the Cornell Notetaking System (any of the variations) as explained in Chapter 4.
The Style	Mark brief, but meaningful phrases. Make jottings brief but in your own words.	Write your notes in full sentences and in your own words, just as you would in an exam.
The Procedure	Finish reading the paragraph or section before taking notes or making any marks. Be extremely selective. Pick out only the essentials from each paragraph. If you try to remember too much you may not remember a thing. Be swift. Read, go back for a mini-overview, and then mark or take notes. Be fast and efficient without being careless. Strive for neatness. Your notes or marks may make sense today, but will they still be readable at the end of the semester?	
Some Tips	Make things a little easier on your memory by putting facts and ideas into categories. Use cross-referencing. If a paragraph reminds you of something you've already read, make a note of it, on both pages.	Don't forget visual materials. Treat them as you would other important facts and ideas, by reviewing and reciting them.

WHAT TO DO WITH EXTRA READINGS

1. Figure out why the book was **assigned**--Know roughly what your'e supposed to get out of the book before you begin.

2. Read the preface--Pay close attention to where the author mentions what makes the book different.

3. Scan the table of contents--Notice how the chapter titles differ from your regular text. Read the information that your book doesn't seem to cover.

4. Read the summary paragraph**s**--These concentrated bits of writing at the end of each chapter should give you a better idea of the book's particular "angle".

5. **Don't leave the book with only vague notions**--Make sure you can say something concrete about it for class discussion or an exam. Know the book's main issues, the author's approach, and other things which make it different from your text. *Think big! Don't get bogged down by details.*

Any other tips on mastering the textbook?   Yes, there's one more important one.

What is it?   It's the Questions-in-the-Margins System, which is similar to the one used with your lecture notes. The System is explained, in step-by-step fashion, in Figure 6.2. Read and study it carefully.

Figure 6.2 System for Reading, Underlining, and Writing Questions.

<table>
<tr><td colspan="2" align="center">QUESTIONS-IN-THE-MARGINS SYSTEM</td></tr>
<tr><td>READ</td><td>Read a small section of a chapter. Might be only half a page, or slightly more; then, stop and go back. Now re-read paragraph by paragraph. Always ask, "What did the author say in this paragraph?"</td></tr>
<tr><td>QUESTION</td><td>Now, in the margin of the page, opposite each paragraph, write a question, or even several questions based on the paragraph.</td></tr>
<tr><td>UNDERLINE</td><td>In each paragraph, underline only the words that will help you to answer the question or questions in the margin. Do not underline anything during the first reading. Underline only after you have formulated the questions. The less underlining, the better!</td></tr>
<tr><td>RECITE</td><td>Finally, using a blank sheet of paper, cover up the printed page, exposing only the questions in the margin. Now, read the question aloud and try to answer it aloud. After reciting, move the sheet down, exposing the paragraph and direct your eyes to the underlined words to check the accuracy of your answer. Repeat this procedure to the end of the chapter.</td></tr>
</table>

One last question: When do you use the reciting step? You recite after you have gone through the entire chapter. At this time you will have the full context of the chapter; thus, when you recite, you'll have a full and vivid picture of the chapter in mind to carry away and reflect on it even while you walk.

MULTIPLE-CHOICE QUIZ

1. You should begin working on your textbook assignments
    a. as early as possible.
    b. during final exams.
    c. the day before classes begin.
    d. the day after classes begin.

2. Get to know your textbook by looking over
    a. the first and second chapters.
    b. the footnotes and the ideas.
    c. the chapter titles, headings and subheadings.
    d. none of the above.

3. The preface is
    a. a boring page that can be skipped.
    b. usually written in a scholarly style.
    c. highly concentrated and packed with facts.
    d. an author's personal statement to the reader.

4. The introduction is
    a. narrow and specific.
    b. well-written.
    c. highly concentrated.
    d. all of the above.

5. Surveying a textbook chapter creates
    a. a number of surprises.
    b. an instant background.
    c. a scattering of facts.
    d. all of the above.

6. One good way to quiz yourself is by turning
    a. chapter titles into answers.
    b. the index into multiple-choice.
    c. headings and subheadings into questions.
    d. none of the above.

7. In the SQ4R method, the 4th R stands for
    a. Read.
    b. Reflect.
    c. Recite.
    d. Record.

8. The chief advantage of marking your textbook is that
    a. the marks cannot be easily erased.
    b. early marks will deemphasize later ones.
    c. your textbook and notebook become one and the same.
    d. key points can be marked with a yellow highlighter.

9. Separate notetaking
    a. is convenient.
    b. takes less time.
    c. creates magnetic centers.
    d. promotes active thinking.

10. Outside readings should be
    a. studied more carefully than your primary text.
    b. studied less carefully than your primary text.
    c. studied with the same care as your primary text.
    d. ignored for the most part.

7
PUTTING YOUR NOTES TO WORK

Now that I have my notes, what should I do with them?   Although taking notes has been proven to aid both concentration and listening skills, its value doesn't stop there. The notes you have are like another textbook, one that you have written yourself. Careful study of this new text will help you to cement the crucial facts of each class securely in your memory.

MASTERING LECTURE NOTES

OK, so how do I put the Cornell System to work?   You can start by going back over your notes and filling in any spaces that you might have left blank.

Fill in
the Blanks

Yes, but what about studying the notes?   Believe it or not, by filling in the blanks, you are studying your notes! In order to know what belongs in the empty spaces you have to reread your notes and understand them. That's the first step in reviewing.

The Recall
Column

What about the recall column I drew on each page?   Up to now, this column should have been empty. Now's the time to read over your notes and try to extract a key word or phrase which will remind you of each important idea. Write this key word in the recall alongside the idea it refers to.

What sort of key words should I use?   Use words or phrases which will remind you of the information on the right side of the page without giving it away completely.

What do I do with the key words?   Once again, the mere act of writing these key words will give you another chance to think about and review your material. However, the value of the key words doesn't stop there. They can now be used to help you remember your notes.

How?   Take a blank sheet of paper and cover up the right-hand side of your note page.

You mean let only the key words show?   That's right. Now read each word or phrase one at a time and recite the information that it refers to.

Reciting

What do you mean by recite?   By recite I mean that you should repeat the information you have learned aloud, from memory and in your own words.

Can't I recite to myself instead?   No. That won't do. If you recite under your breath or silently there is too great a chance that you will skip over ideas that you have trouble with. If you recite out loud it will be almost impossible for you to fake it. An incorrect or incomplete answer should stick out like a sore thumb.

A General
Overview

Is that all I need to do in order to review a lecture?   There's one last step. After you've recited every page using the procedure described, pull out all of your notes from the lecture and overlap them so that only the recall columns are exposed. Now run your eyes down each column from the first page to the last. This brief glance at the recall columns should provide you with a powerful sense of the lecture as a whole.

Is one thorough review good enough to remember the lecture for the entire semester?   Unfortunately, the answer is no. Forgetting is too powerful an enemy to be defeated with just one review session. However, a quick run through of your notes from time to time should provide you with the necessary reinforcements to put up a good fight.

MASTERING YOUR TEXTBOOK

Textbook
Reciting

Is the procedure for mastering textbook material any different?   Yes. With textbook assignments, you have the unique opportunity to recite as you read. After each paragraph, before you write anything down, cover up the page and try to recite what you have just read. If you can't you should probably re-read that paragraph. Otherwise, take notes as you normally would.

Is there any other advantage to reciting a textbook that you won't get in reciting lecture notes?   Yes. There are four advantages to reciting your textbook.

The Advantages of Reciting Your Textbook

- Promotes concentration.
- Forms a basis for understanding the next paragraph.
- Gives your memory some time to consolidate what you've just learned.
- Provides immediate feedback on how you're doing.

How much time should I spend reciting?   Studies show that the more you recite, the more you learn.

Do you mean I should spend more time reciting than reading? Definitely. Reading and studying are not the same. Reading just provides you with the raw material for study. That material must be processed by recitation.

Re-reading *Isn't re-reading the textbook a better method of reviewing?*   That's a common myth that spells trouble. Here's why: Key ideas are often missed or misunderstood on the first reading. The sad fact is re-reading seldom fills in these missing pieces. In other words, with re-reading, little or no learning takes place. In order to learn efficiently you must take a different approach; and that approach is reciting.

What about writing instead of reciting?   Writing is not a bad idea, assuming you have time. But don't write instead of reciting. Do both so you can learn three ways at once: with your eyes, your ears and the muscles of your writing hand.

LATER REVIEWS

Does it make sense to review my notes from time to time?   Yes. It makes plenty of sense. Don't think that just because you've worked on an assignment once that you are set for the semester. Studying an assignment is alot like taking care of a car: both need constant maintenance. So give your notes a tune-up with periodic reviews.

Should these later reviews be done like immediate reviews? You can start the same way, that is, by reciting. However, you can better organize your information at this point by categorizating it. Any time you put information in categories, you'll have a better chance of remembering it.

Categori-
zation

What sort of categories should I use? That depends on the subject of course. As a general rule, try to make up categories which improve not only your memory but your knowledge as well. For example, don't put Bach, Beethoven, and Brahms under a category "composers whose names begin with B," although it's true that they all do. Instead, categorize them under the heading "German composers" so you can organize your information and learn from it at the same time.

REFLECTION

Reviewing
vs.
Reflecting

What's the difference between reflecting and reviewing? Reviewing means going over information that you already know. Reflecting involves taking the information you know a step further, examining its implications and reading between the lines.

But information that's between the lines is seldom covered in exams. You're wrong there. Reading between the lines can be the essence of an essay question. Furthermore, reflection can give you a greater understanding of your subject so that even objective questions, like multiple-choice and true-false, will seem easier.

How do I go about reflecting on something? The best way is to take what you have read or listened to and ask yourself some broader questions.

Can you give me an example of some good questions? Sure, here are several.

Questions You Can Use For Reflection

Here are some general questions which should help you to begin reflecting on your lectures and textbook assignments:

1. What is the significance of these facts or ideas?
2. What principle are they based on?
3. What else could they be applied to?
4. How do they fit in with what I already know?
5. What can I see that lies beyond these facts and ideas but is still based upon them?

Isn't reflection kind of time-consuming?   Not at all. In fact, reflection is very time efficient. Unlike reviewing which requires notes and/or a textbook, reflection, needs only an inquisitive mind. Therefore you can reflect while you're exercising, while you're walking to and from classes, or even while you're waiting in line. These are all times that you might otherwise have wasted by staring into space, daydreaming or worst of all, worrying.

MULTIPLE-CHOICE QUIZ

1. A good set of notes can function as a second
    a. teacher.
    b. textbook.
    c. memory.
    d. margin.

2. Key words in the recall column should be used as
    a. answers.
    b. explanations.
    c. reminders.
    d. assignments.

3. The best way to get a general overview of your notes is by
    a. overlapping them, leaving only the recall columns exposed.
    b. re-reading them as quickly as you can.
    c. covering the recall columns and reciting the notes.
    d. constructing a brief quiz made up of main ideas.

4. Textbook mastery is unique because
    a. most of the work has been done for you.
    b. you are able to recite as you read.
    c. modern texts contain glossaries and quizzes.
    d. you are able to recite in your own words.

5. Textbook reciting
    a. permits consolidation.
    b. promotes concentration.
    c. provides immediate feedback.
    d. all of the above.

6. In general, when compared to total textbook reading time, total textbook *reciting* time
    a. should be longer.
    b. should be shorter.
    c. should be equal.
    d. will vary depending upon the text.

7. Re-reading your text is a bad way to review because
    a. it often fails to fill gaps in understanding.
    b. it repeats the same approach over and over.
    c. very little true learning takes place.
    d. all of the above.

8. Later reviews
    a. should be saved until exam time.
    b. will seldom help to battle forgetting.
    c. should be used as "tune-ups" for assignments.
    d. are no different than immediate reviews.

9. Categorization should be used to
    a. better organize your notes.
    b. improve your memory.
    c. enhance your knowledge.
    d. all of the above.

10. Reflection
    a. involves going over information you already know.
    b. is enriching, but largely impractical in tests.
    c. develops skills that are important in writing essays.
    d. is the main component of textbook recitation.

8
PREPARING FOR EXAMS

ADVANCE PREPARATION

When should I start to prepare for exams?

At the very beginning of the semester. Exam preparation begins with a faithful attendance of lectures and a dependable completion of assignments.

How about the really intense studying?

About a week before exams you should shift into overdrive by finishing up any back assignments and by beginning your extensive review of the semester's material. The best way to accomplish all of this is with a time schedule.

What should I include in my time schedule?

Divide the entire week into half-hour time blocks. Begin by filling in the time taken up by meals, sleep, exercise, job (if you have one) and classes. Then use the time that remains to finish any old assignments so the decks will be clear when exam week arrives.

Is it okay to miss class in order to study for exams?

No. Although it's never a good idea to miss classes, now is a particularly bad time. Your instructor will often use the last few classes to sum up the course as a whole and to answer any questions about the upcoming exam.

Should I have an exam week schedule as well?

Of course. Once again, begin by filling in meals, sleep and exercise. Carefully mark off your exam periods and then set off a block of time directly before each exam for one last review. Use the rest of the time to study for your other exams.

SUMMARY SHEETS

Is there any special procedure for reviewing?

Yes. You can take the categorizing used in later reviews a step further with what are known as summary sheets.

What are summary sheets?

They're distilled versions of your lecture and textbook notes.

What are their advantages?

There are three distinct ones. 1) Making up your summary sheets will give you a final thorough review of a semester's worth of notes. 2) The categorizing that you do will enable you to organize your notes in a form that is easier to remember. 3) The finished product, the summary, sheets themselves, will provide you with an efficient homemade study guide.

How do I make up these summary sheets?

Go back through your notes and pick out the most important facts from each lecture and textbook assignment. As you do so, make an effort to organize this information into categories that will help you remember it. Write your categorized notes on paper that has been ruled for the Cornell Notetaking System.

What sort of categories should I use?

Try to arrange your information in a form that is different from the way you first learned it. For example, if your history book takes a chronological approach you might try organizing your notes under headings which emphasize themes instead of time. Figure 8.1 is a summary sheet from a course on 20th Century American Culture. Although the instructor delivered the information in chronological order, the student has arranged the facts about the motion picture industry under the categories: audiences, theaters, and social content.

How many summary sheets will I need?

You'll want one set of summary sheets for your textbook notes and another for your lecture notes. Try to keep each set to ten pages or less.

What about all that material that I'll have to leave out?

It would be close to impossible for you to remember everything you've learned. Furthermore, if you try, you run the risk of overloading your brain and drawing a blank. It makes far more sense to pick and choose the most important ideas.

Do I still put a recall column in my summary sheets?

Yes. And, as you've done in the past, you should go back through these sheets and write in key words for the important facts.

Should I recite my summary sheets?

Yes. Now that your summary sheets are complete, the procedure for reciting them is the same as you've been using all along. The difference, of course, is that instead of a single lecture or textbook chapter, you'll be studying the "best" of an entire semester.

CRAMMING

Are you against cramming?

I'm not *against* cramming. At times it is an unfortunate necessity. My feeling is that if you must cram then you should do so efficiently. Efficient cramming requires real courage.

Why courage?

You need courage in order to resist trying to memorize too much material. You must select only a handful of facts even at the risk of leaving out something important.

Why should I leave out something important?

Because if you've reached the point where you have to cram, you really have no other choice. If you try to stuff yourself with facts it's like stuffing yourself with food: there's a good chance that you won't retain a thing.

Why can't I just memorize until time runs out?

That's dangerous. By trying to memorize too much, you'll wind up doing a poor job of memorizing anything. Studies show that upon hitting the first tough question, the entire flimsy fabric of facts may collapse, resulting in chaos and confusion, and making it difficult to salvage anything from the wreckage.

Wouldn't an all-nighter be the answer?

No. You'll drag into the exam with a tired mind and body, the worst possible situation. You may be able to answer some questions on reflex, but on questions that require genuine thought, you're liable to draw a blank.

Figure 8.1 Summary Sheet

20th Century Amer Culture - Prof. Owens

Motion Picture Industry

Audiences

I. Audiences

1905 interest
demand →
creativity

from 1905 on — interest in movies increased
public demand stimulated creativity

1938 - 80 mil. attend

1938 - 80 million movie admissions per week

1973 - less than 20

1973 - less than 20 million

Theaters

II. Theaters

Moguls - immigrants

Most of the first movie moguls were Jewish immigrants, often nickelodeon owners

Features → big theaters

Birth of feature film lead to lavish theaters

"Block-booking" - monopoly

"Block-booking" - some studios would monopolize theaters by making an "all-or-nothing" arrangement.

Double-feature after Depression
(games & giveaways too)

Double-feature — effort to increase attendance after the Depression

Halftime games (bingo, etc) and giveaways were also common ploy

Crowds, TV - end big theaters

Dwindling crowds and advent of TV brought end to large theaters

Social content

III. Social Content

Early eroticism → star system

Eroticism and scandal on and offscreen were linked to Hollywood "star system"

Hays (1934)

Hays Office (1934) sought to clamp down on movie immorality.

"gentle propaganda"

Movies of '30's and '40's preached "gentle propaganda" of optimism and wholesomeness.

WWII movies - 2 kinds

2 kinds of movies during WWII - "Escapist" to ease pain of war and "propagandist" to bolster patriotism

Post-war: Racy adaptations

Post war: Racier themes came back to movies by way of novel and play adaptations

50's Westerns used mythic settings to discuss/critique modern American values.

Corruption of crooks and kids

Corruption in 50's and 60's - loveable gangsters became psychotic. Kids became rebellious.

Can cramming replace regular study?

Never! As you can see, cramming involves a sacrifice. It is an emergency measure designed to pull you through an exam with a passing grade. It is a technique for survival, not success.

EXAM DAY

What should I do to get ready on exam day?

Get there early so you can find a good seat where you can hear the proctor, see the board and stay away from friends.

Avoid friends? Why?

Even the best of friends is nothing but a distraction in an exam. With a friend nearby you may be tempted to chat instead of doing any last minute studying. You might also be inclined to rush through your exam in order to finish at the same time. Finally, any eye contact the two of you make could look like cheating.

Exams make me tense. Is their anything I can do about that?

You can use the Doctor's Method. It was originally designed for patients with high blood pressure, but it has also been proven to reduce common tension.

The Doctor's Method For Reducing Tension

1. Breathe in until your lungs feel completely full.
2. Now take a sudden, extra breath through your mouth.
3. Let your breath out slowly.

Repeat this procedure seven times.

Should I start answering questions right away?

No. There are a number of things you should do before you pick up your pen or pencil.

Before You Start Writing...

1. Read and listen to directions. Be aware of the written directions as well as any others given orally.

2. Skim the exam. Take a minute or two to look over the exam so you know what you'll be encountering.

3. Plan your time. Now that you know the directions and have a rough idea of what the questions are like, decide how much time you'll spend on each question. Then check your watch now and then to see that you're still on schedule.

Now you're ready to begin the exam.

Should I answer the difficult questions first so I've got them out of the way?

No. Go for the easy ones first. If you target the tough questions, you may find yourself both discouraged and low on time. Answering the easier questions first should give you confidence and create momentum as well.

What if there's a question that I can't answer?

Sometimes it helps to re-read a difficult question. However, if nothing clicks on the second reading, then move on to the next question. You may have time to come back to any tough ones at the end of the exam.

Should I leave any answers blank?

Not unless there's a penalty for wrong answers. Obviously an answer left blank is going to do you no real good at all. In most cases it's best to hazard a guess.

What if I finish the exam with time to spare?

By all means, use that time. Don't waste it. Go back over any questions you might have skipped and give them a second try. Also, look for any careless mistakes.

MULTIPLE-CHOICE QUIZ

1. Exam preparation begins
    a. at the start of the semester.
    b. with faithful attendance of lectures.
    c. with dependable completion of assignments.
    d. all of the above.

2. The key to an efficient exam week is
    a. careful recitation.
    b. a time schedule.
    c. exercise.
    d. completing your assignments.

3. Summary sheets are
    a. a further example of categorization.
    b. distilled versions of your notes.
    c. a valuable exam study tool.
    d. all of the above.

4. Your summary sheets should
    a. be longer than your notes.
    b. be written in the Cornell format.
    c. contain details that your notes didn't mention.
    d. combine your lecture and textbook notes.

5. Writing your summary sheets requires
    a. picking and choosing.
    b. legal-sized paper.
    c. a conference with the instructor.
    d. all of the above.

6. Cramming is
    a. for cowards.
    b. always inefficient.
    c. sometimes an unfortunate necessity.
    d. a way to combat memory overload.

7. The "Doctor's Method" is a technique for
    a. reducing test anxiety.
    b. raising blood pressure.
    c. arranging your textbook notes.
    d. answering objective test questions.

8. Before you start on your exam, you should
    a. read and listen to directions.
    b. skim the exam.
    c. plan out your time.
    d. all of the above.

9. Easy exam questions should be
    a. saved as a "reward."
    b. answered first.
    c. outlined in the margin.
    d. used to reduce momentum.

10. Answers should be left blank
    a. only if they're multiple-choice.
    b. only if the question is a trick one.
    c. only if there's a strong penalty for wrong answers.
    d. under no circumstances.

9
OBJECTIVE TESTS

TRUE-FALSE

Is there a typical true-false question?

Most true-false questions tend to fit into the following pattern: They are made up of two things or qualities and their relationship such as "Tests create anxiety" or "Smoke indicates fire."

The idea of choosing true or false seems so easy. What makes it so difficult?

Qualifiers.

Qualifiers

What are qualifiers?

They're words like *all, most* and *some*. They make statements more specific and as a result make them more complex.

*Are **all, most** and **some** the only qualifiers?*

No, there are really six basic families of qualifiers. *All, most* and *some* belong to only one of these six groups. It would be a good idea to memorize these six sets of qualifiers.

Six Sets of Qualifiers

<u>A</u>ll - *most - some - none*
<u>A</u>lways - *usually - sometimes - never*
<u>G</u>reat - *much - little - no*
<u>M</u>ore - *equal - less*
<u>G</u>ood - *bad*
<u>I</u>s - *is not*

What's the point of learning these qualifiers by heart?

If you memorize these qualifiers then you can mentally run through the list whenever you encounter a true-false question.

What good will that do?

Knowing these qualifiers will give you a chance to play Goldilocks. You'll be able to determine which qualifier understates the sentence, which one overstates the sentence and which one makes it just right.

Using Qualifiers to Solve A True-False Question

1. Find the qualifier in the true-false statement.
2. Decide which set the qualifier belongs to.
3. Mentally replace the qualifier with each member of the qualifier set.
4. If none of the replacements seems to make the sentence true then the statement was probably true in the first place.
5. If one of the qualifiers does seem to make the sentence true then the original statement is probably false.

100 Percent Words

Is that all I need to know in order to solve true-false questions?

Unfortunately, no. There are a couple of other aspects of true-false questions that are likely to give you trouble. One such aspect is 100 percent words. These are the qualifiers which say that a question is true without exception.

Some 100 Percent Words

no	*every*	*entirely*	*best*
never	*always*	*only*	*worst*
none	*all*	*invariably*	

Give me an example of a question with a 100 percent word.

Take a look at the statement below:

Self-winding watches *never* stop running.

In this sentence the 100% word is *never*. Although self-winding watches are designed to run without winding, shock or water may cause a watch of this type to stop. Therefore, the statement is false.

What should I do when I find a statement which contains a 100 percent word?

Be suspicious. These statements won't always be false but there's a good chance of it. Therefore, if you run low on time and you read a statement with a 100 percent word you may want to make it false.

Are 100 percent words ever part of a true statement?

Yes they are. Although the cases are rare, there are enough of them around to prevent you from automatically marking any statement with a 100% word false.

In-Between Words

Are there any other qualifiers that I should be looking out for?

Yes. In-between words. These words tend to call for a compromise.

Some In-Between Words

usually	*often*	*generally*
seldom	*many*	*frequently*
sometimes	*most*	*ordinarily*
few	*some*	

What's the rule with in-between words?

Just the opposite from 100% words. Because these words fall in between the two extremes, they are usually true. But beware, as in the case of the 100% words, there are some exceptions.

Long Statements

Why are long statements often false?

In order for a statement to be true, every part of it must be true. It follows then that as a sentence grows longer, the chances increase that part of it will be false.

Are there any other variations of this partially true type sentence?

Yes. Sometimes you will run into a sentence that is made up of two true statements and yet its overall meaning is false.

How can that be?

It is possible for two true statements to lead to a false conclusion, as in the following example. This emphasizes the need to read each true-false statement both carefully and completely. The following sentence is made up of two statements that are true. However, the word *because* draws a false conclusion and, as a result, the entire sentence is false.

Beware of False Logic

True: Wolfgang Amadeus Mozart was a child prodigy.
True: Mozart died when he was 35.
False: Wolfgang Amadeus Mozart was a child prodigy *because* he died when he was 35.

Negatives

What do you mean by negatives?

Negatives in a true-false statement can be more than just *no* and *not*. They can also be prefixes which turn a word into its opposite as in *legal* and *illegal, happy* and *unhappy.*

What's the quickest way to determine whether a statement with negatives is false or true?

Pull out all of the negatives and see if the statement that remains is true or false. Now count up your negatives (both words and prefixes). If their number is even than the statement is the same as the one with no negatives. If the number is odd then the statement is the opposite of the statement with no negatives.

True-False Questions With Negatives

1. Circle the negatives and negative prefixes in the sentence and count them.

   There is no law in the state of Maryland which says that it is not illegal to exceed a posted speed limit.

   Total number of negatives and negative prefixes: 3 (odd)

2. Read the sentence without the negatives and decide if it is true or false:

   There is [a] law in the state of Maryland which says that it is legal to exceed a posted speed limit.

   This sentence is FALSE.

3. If the number of negatives is even then the original statement's meaning is the same as the statement above. If the number of negatives is odd then the meaning of the original statement is the opposite of the statement above.

   Therefore, the original statement is TRUE.

Is it worth guessing on a true-false question?

Yes. But don't do it by flipping a coin. Guess intelligently. Here are two guidelines for guessing:

Guidelines For Guessing

1. **Most true-false tests contain more true statements than false ones.** That's because your instructor wants you to remember information that is accurate.
2. **Guessing pays off even if points are taken off for each wrong answer.** No test question has better odds. Each true-false question gives you a fifty-fifty chance to begin with. If you know something about the subject, your odds improve.

MULTIPLE CHOICE

How are most multiple-choice questions written?

The most common multiple-choice questions involve an incomplete sentence or *stem* followed by four or five choices known as *options*. The incorrect options are called *decoys* or *distractions*.

The Elements of A Multiple-Choice Question

stem   In 1939, the Academy Award for "Best Picture went to

distractors   a. *The Wizard of Oz.*
or decoys   b. *Pride of the Yankees.*
                              c. *2001: A Space Odyssey.*   *options*
correct   d. *Gone With the Wind.*
option

Will only the correct option complete the sentence?

No. That's what makes things tough. In a well-written multiple-choice question, *all* of the options will complete the sentence but only one will do so *correctly*.

What's the procedure for answering a multiple-choice question?

One way to pick up points on a multiple-choice test is to be methodical. Here are four steps which should help.

Answering A Multiple-Choice Question

1. Read the directions.
2. Read the stem all the way through.
3. Read every single option.
4. Choose the best option.

What if I can't answer the question right away?

Skip it for now. It makes no sense to let a single question run you out of both time and patience. Go on to the next question. You can often come back to a troublesome problem if you have extra time. Just be sure to mark any options that you've managed to eliminate before you move on. That way you won't have to start over completely when you come back.

The Second Time Around

Should I handle the question any differently on the second time around?

Yes. This time, if you haven't already, make a definite effort to eliminate one or two options.

How difficult is it to eliminate one or two options?

Not as difficult as you might think. There are some ways that you can eliminate options even if you don't know your material. And, of course, there are even surer ways of narrowing options if you *do* know your material.

If You Don't Know Your Material

How can I get rid of options if I don't know the material?

Although multiple-choice questions may vary widely, there are a number of clues which can help to lead you to the correct option.

Narrowing Your Choices If You Don't Know The Material

1. *Watch out for 100% words.*   As we learned from true-false, these words are seldom to be trusted.
2. *Get rid of foolish options.*   Some instructors fill spaces with foolish options. Although these options are sometimes amusing, they are always give-aways.
3. *"All of the above" is usually correct.*   The "all of the above" option is an attractive one. That's because it allows the instructor to give you several facts instead of just one. Therefore, if in doubt, pick "all of the above."
4. *The long answer is seldom wrong.*   Unlike in true-false questions where the long answer is suspect, long answers in multiple-choice often mean that the instructor has over qualified the correct option in order to insure that it is completely correct.
5. *Check for look-alikes.*   Look-alikes are answers which differ by only a word or two. More often than not they show where the instructor's interests lie. If you spot a pair of look-alikes, chances are good that one of these two answers is going to be the correct one.
6. *Pick a number in the middle range.*   In a question that has numbers for answers, instructors tend to bracket the correct response with at least one number higher and one number lower. So if you're stumped, toss out the high and low numbers and choose from the ones that remain.

If You Do Know Your Material

What are the methods for narrowing when I do know my material?

Here are three strategies:

Strategies To Use When You Know Your Material

USE THE TRUE-FALSE TECHNIQUE.-Most multiple-choice questions can be thought of as a series of true-false statements. Simply join the stem with each option. When you decide which statement is true, you will have selected the correct option.

STICK TO THE SUBJECT MATTER.-Don't let unfamiliar options make you apprehensive. If you know your material you should realize whether an option sticks to the subject matter. If it doesn't, then get rid of it, and make your job that much easier.

WATCH OUT FOR NEGATIVES.-A small word like *no* or prefix like *non-* or *il-* can be easily overlooked. Yet these and other negatives can make a world of difference in a multiple-choice question. Don't take chances! Circle any negative words or prefixes that you come across.

MATCHING

What does the standard matching test look like?

Normally it will have two vertical lines of randomly organized items placed side by side. Often, but not always, the items in one list will be briefer than those in the other. The task is to connect an item from one list to an item from the other. The directions will tell what sort of relationship should exist between the two.

What are the steps for answering a matching question?

A calm, well-organized approach is best for a matching question. The following three steps should help to insure this:

How To Take A Matching Test

1. Read the directions--Matching directions may vary.
2. Glance down both columns--Become familiar with the material before you make your first match.
3. Read the top left item and then match it with the items in the right hand column--Don't go back and forth in a haphazard way. Be methodical.

If I've found a match should I go on?

No. Keep looking to be sure you've got the best match for that item. As a rule, check every choice before you make a connection. One incorrect match can lead to several wrong answers and at times can actually sabotage an entire matching test.

What if I'm not sure that the match is a good one?

Avoid the domino effect that can result by matching a wrong answer. Instead, go on to the next item and try to make a match for it. Each time you make a sure match you narrow the choices for those matches which give you trouble.

Figure 9.1   The Matching System in Action

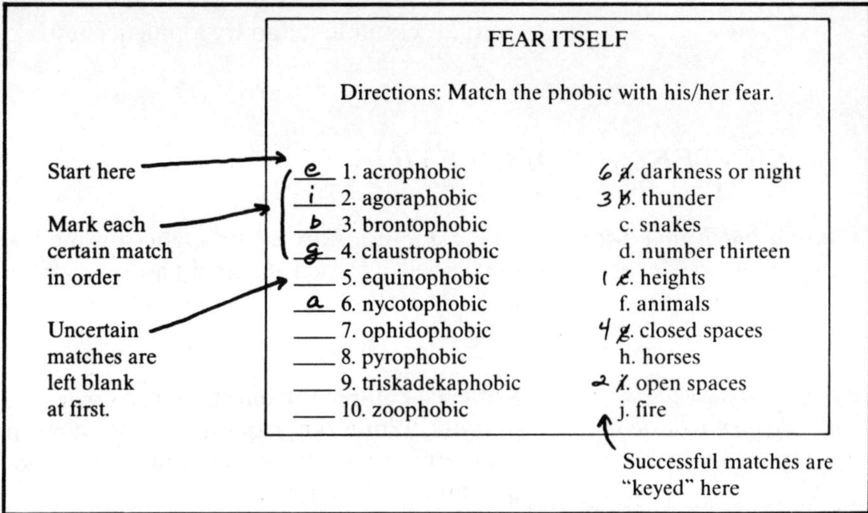

Any other hints that will make answering a matching question a little easier?

Some sort of marking system can be a help. For example, you might want to circle the letter or number alongside each match as you use it. That way you'll have a better idea of the choices that remain. [See Figure 9.1]

Studying for Matching Tests

How about studying for a matching test. Is there any way that I can prepare?

If you have an idea that your exam is going to include a matching question (you might try asking the instructor directly) you can start to study for it almost immediately by keeping a running list of all the terms and definitions that might show up on a matching test.

Should I prepare my own practice matching test?

Not right away at least. A better idea is to line up two columns of terms and definitions in the proper order. Then cover one column and see if you can recite each item by using a matching item in the exposed column for clues.

That sounds a lot like the Cornell System.

That's no coincidence. A matching test is like two cue columns. Once you've recited the list several times, reverse the process by uncovering the other column this time and reciting the column you've just read. Finally, when you feel that you've mastered the material you might want to scramble it and try a practice test.

SENTENCE-COMPLETION

I have a tough time with sentence-completion. There are no answers to choose from.

These questions are even tougher for the test-maker because each statement must be written in such a way that only one answer will be correct.

If they're so difficult to make up then why do instructors bother with them?

Sentence-completion questions serve a definite purpose. While other question types concentrate on recognition, sentence-completion questions test your recall.

Recognition vs. Recall

What is recognition?

With recognition, the answer is there. All you have to do is pick it out.

And recall?

With recall the emphasis is put on memory. The answer must come from your brain. It's not just a matter of pick and choose.

The Typical Sentence-Completion Question

What does a typical completion-type question look like?

The typical sentence-completion question is a grammatical sentence in which one of the words has been replaced by a blank. Of course, if the blank happens to come at the end (or at the very beginning), your job is relatively easy. You've got the continuous context of the entire sentence to help you choose your answer. If the blank comes anywhere else then things get a little more difficult.

A TYPICAL SENTENCE-COMPLETION QUESTION
In 1945, Franklin Roosevelt, Winston Churchill and Joseph Stalin held a wartime conference in the Ukranian city of _______________.

[The answer is *Yalta.*]

Two-Blank Statements

How do I cope with two blanks?

Two blanks aren't really harder than one blank questions, just a little different. There are actually two variations of a two-blank sentence. 1) The blanks can be consecutive or 2) they can be widely separated.

What do I do if the blanks are consecutive?

Generally you'll want to think up a name because that's what two consecutive blanks are usually asking for. Just knowing that can be a great relief.

Will the length of the blanks help me to narrow my choices even further?

No. The length of the blanks will almost never have any relation to the name that belongs in them. For example, two short blanks could just as easily hold "Tom Thumb" as they could "Christopher Columbus" even though the lengths of the two names vary greatly.

What about when the blanks are separated?

The best procedure here is to treat each blank as though it appears in a separate sentence. Far too many students make the mistake of trying to connect the missing words in some way even though they may not be related.

Long Blanks

Don't some sentences have extra long blanks?

Yes. If there is only one blank and it is especially long, it's safe to assume the testmaker is looking for a phrase or clause.

Is this type of question very common?

No, actually. Questions which ask for a phrase instead of a word are difficult to grade because there can be some many different "correct" answers.

Question-Answering Strategies

Are there any clues that will help me to find the answer to a sentence-completion?

Because sentence-completion questions call on your recall rather than your recognition, there will be no clues which, point to specific answers. However, you can use grammar as well as some carefully phrased questions to narrow things down a bit.

How is grammar going to help?

Because your blank occurs in a sentence it must follow the rules of grammar, just as any other word in the sentence. In the following example, the key to the sentence is the word *misses.* It indicates that the answer is singular, which means, of course, that you have only one choice.

An average of ________________ out of every four Americans misses breakfast regularly.

What about "a" and "an"?

Although it is second nature for most of us, there is a definite rule about the use of the articles *a* and *an. A* is used before nouns that begin with consonants while *an* is used before nouns which begin with vowels. Knowing this can help to narrow your choices down if the word before the blank is *a* or *an.* [The correct answer is *one.]*

An ________________ is defined as 160 square rods or 4,840 square yards.

In the above example, the word *an* eliminates many words that may have been considered as possibilities. Foot, furlong, range and mile all will not fit because the *an* indicates that the answer must begin with a vowel. [The correct answer is *acre.*]

The Question-Asking Strategy

What's the question-asking strategy?

That's a straightforward method for eliminating any confusion that might be built into the sentence-completion. The solution is a simple one: If you don't understand, ask! The difficult part is arriving at a question which will provide you with a satisfactory answer. You'll want to ask a precise question which clears up exactly what you need to know instead of a vague question which is apt to receive a vague response in return. In that sense, you're in the same boat as the testmaker. Just ask carefully and you'll do fine.

Guessing

Is there a special procedure for guessing on a sentence-completion?

Yes, there is. Although guessing isn't tremendously successful with sentence-completion it is always better to guess on a question than to take a zero for it.

Procedure For Guessing on Sentence-Completion Questions

1. Go through the entire test first, answering only the questions you are sure of.
2. Mark the questions that you are unable to answer.
3. On the second pass, read each unanswered question over again.
4. If you are still unable to answer it, make a guess, based on common sense, as to what you think the answer should be.

MULTIPLE-CHOICE QUIZ

1. True-false questions are complicated by
    a. qualifiers.
    b. relationships.
    c. verbs.
    d. all of the above.

2. Words which claim that a statement is true without exception are know as
    a. In-between Words.
    b. 100% Percent Words.
    c. qualifiers.
    d. understatements.

3. Longer true-false statements usually
    a. emphasize false logic.
    b. have a greater chance of being true.
    c. have a greater chance of being false.
    d. need only to be partially true.

4. The best way to approach a true-false statement with negatives is to
    a. first read the sentence without the negatives.
    b. determine if the negatives are words or prefixes.
    c. measure the length of the statement.
    d. all of the above.

5. In a well-written multiple-choice question, the distractors
    a. are also known as the stems.
    b. are the same as qualifiers.
    c. will make the statement correct.
    d. will complete the sentence.

6. If you are forced to guess on a multiple-choice question, you should probably *not* eliminate an option which
    a. contains 100% words.
    b. seems foolish or silly.
    c. is longer than the rest.
    d. features the largest quantity.

7. A multiple-choice question can be thought of as a series of
    a. matching questions.
    b. essay questions.
    c. true-false questions.
    d. none of the above.

8. Before you make your first match in a matching test, it is important to
    a. read the directions.
    b. become familiar with the material.
    c. make sure you have the *best* match.
    d. all of the above.

9. A good way to study for a matching test is to
    a. memorize sets of qualifiers.
    b. extract key words and terms from your notes.
    c. develop a foolproof system of marking.
    d. avoid the domino effect.

10. Unlike other objective tests, sentence-completion requires
    a. recognition.
    b. reflection.
    c. recall.
    d. review.

10
ESSAY TESTS

SHORT ANSWER QUESTIONS

Why do you have a section on short-answer tests in a chapter on essay questions?

Although short-answers are often mentioned in the same breath with true-false and multiple-choice questions, they are really more like mini essays. Like an essay, with a short-answer you can give a variety of responses and still be correct.

How can I become a good short-answer testtaker?

Here are some guidelines:

How To Answer A Short Answer Question

1. *Think before you write*--That way you can be sure you are using your words efficiently.
2. *Give direct answers*--Your main goal is to present information.
3. *Use telegraphic sentences*--It's the facts, not the frills that count. If your instructor requires complete sentences, make them short and to the point.
4. *Work through the test twice*--On the first pass, answer only the questions you are sure of. Mark the questions you have skipped. On your second trip, rethink the troublesome questions and write down any fragments you can recall. If these bits and pieces are put in a logical order you are more apt to receive credit.

ESSAY QUESTIONS

And what about essay questions?	With essays the procedure is remarkably similar. The major differences have to do with the fact that an essay answer is often many times longer than a short-answer response.
What's the first step in taking an essay exam?	Preparation. You want to be in a proper mental set for the exam, or as professional athletes say, you want to be *psyched up*. Here are some questions which should help you.

Getting "Psyched Up" For An Essay Exam

1. What type of question is the instructor most likely to ask?
2. What type of question has caused me the most trouble in the past?
3. What sort of grade do I need to get and what do I want to accomplish with this exam?
4. How is the time limit of the exam as well as the format going to affect my intentions?
5. What kind of question do I want to answer?

What's the first thing I should do once the exam has been handed out?	Empty your mind. If you're like most people you'll walk into an exam with dozens of thoughts swirling around in your head. Now is the time to write down on the back of the exam paper any ideas that you would like to work into your exam answers. With the important ideas on paper you can clear your mind of anything else that remains. That way your mind will be free to do the organizing and reasoning necessary for answering an essay question.
What else can I do before I begin to write my exam?	Here are four more suggestions:

Before You Answer Any Questions...

1. Read the directions. Don't make the mistake of doing more or less work than you had to, simply because you didn't take a minute or two to read the directions.

2. Read all questions.   Know what you'll be answering before you actually begin. This is a great help especially if you're asked to pick out the questions you want to answer.

3. Jot down any ideas.   As you read each question, your empty mind should begin filling up with ideas again. Don't rely on your memory. As ideas occur to you, jot them down in the margin next to the question that they refer to. You may also want to circle key words in the question.

4. Budget your time.   You won't have time to make out a time chart on paper but you can have a mental plan of how much time you're going to devote to each question.

Answering The Essay Question

How can I improve the way I actually answer essay questions?

You can start by understanding the question with precision. A vague understanding inevitably leads to a vague answer.

Yes, but the questions themselves are often so vague.

Not true. Most of the terms in an essay question have very specific meanings. The list below provides brief definitions for some common essay terms. Figure 10.1 provides a comparison of a few of these terms.

KEY WORDS IN ESSAY QUESTIONS

Apply principle--Show how principle works through an example.

Comment--Discuss briefly.

Compare--Emphasize similarities but also differences.

Contrast--Give only the differences.

Criticize--Give your judgments, as to good points, drawbacks.

Define--Supply meanings without details.

Describe--State in detail, the particulars.

Demonstrate--Show or prove your opinion, evaluation, or judgment.

Diagram--Show drawing with labels.

Differentiate--Show how two things are different.

Discuss--Give reasons, pro and con, with details.

Distinguish--Show main points between two things, how different.

Enumerate--List the points.

Evaluate--Discuss advantages and disadvantages; your opinion, too.

Identify--Describe events, places, or persons.

Illustrate--Give an example.

Interpret--Give your judgment.

Justify--Prove or give reasons.

List--List without details.

Outline--Make a short summary of heads and subheads.

Purpose--Tell how something fulfills the overall design.

Prove--Give evidence and reasons.

Relate--Show how things inter-connect.

Review--Show main points or events in summary form.

Show--List your evidence in order of time, importance, logic.

State--List main points briefly, without details.

Summarize--Organize and bring together main points only.

Solve--Come up with your solution from given facts.

Support--Back up your statements with facts and proof.

Trace--Give main points from beginning to end of an event.

Figure 10.1 Be sure to comply with a question's specific directions.

1. Define "hypercharge"

Hypercharge is a theoretical fifth force which acts on objects of different composition.

2. Interpret the overall effect that the theoretical fifth force, known as "hypercharge," would have on physics.

If the existance of the fifth force, hypercharge, is confirmed, it will have a revolutionary effect on physics. The findings of such highly respected physicists as Galileo and Einstein will most likely

3. Support or refute this statement: "If the existence of a fifth force, hypercharge, is proven, it will have a dramatic effect on modern physics."

I support the notion that, if proven, hypercharge will have a dramatic effect on modern physics. The existance of hypercharge will undermine Galileo's wide-

What if I still can't figure out what the question means?

If your head can't do the job then use your hand. Raise it and when you're called on, ask a well-phrased question to straighten out your confusion.

How long should each essay be?

Length isn't really important. It's completeness that matters. I realize that there's always someone at an exam who goes through test booklets faster than a builder goes through nails. Don't get caught up in the competition. Rambling won't win you points. A well-written essay will. So make your essay as long as it needs to be in order for your reasoning to be clear. Remember of course, that you do have a limited amount of time.

Should I get the tough questions out of the way first?

No. The routine's the same with almost all tests: Answer the easy questions first. That way you'll have time--and momentum, on your side.

I guess an essay answer has to be well-organized.

You bet. Not only that but it must *look* well-organized. It may surprise you to learn that many graders are more concerned about how your answer is *written* than what you actually *write*.

You mean I could pass an essay exam without learning the material?

I'm afraid not. You won't get away with a well-organized essay that says nothing. The content of your essay is still crucial. The point is that you can do poorly on an essay question, even if you know the material inside and out, if what you have written isn't well-organized.

How should I organize my answer?

Overall organization will usually depend upon subject matter as well as personal taste. However, if you follow this rule: *ONE IDEA–ONE PARAGRAPH* you'll do a good job of keeping your answer on track.

Is it okay to add the personal touch to my answers, that is, give an opinion?

As a general rule, leave out personal opinions. Your instructor wants to know what you've *learned* not how you *feel*.

Can I use accepted opinions other than my own?

Yes, but only if you support them. For example, you can't just write that "Baltimore is the most liveable major city in the U.S." You must say "According to the January 1987 issue of *Life*, Baltimore is the most liveable major city in the U.S."

Is bad handwriting going to hurt me at all?

I'm afraid so. Although graders try to be objective, it's difficult not to be negatively affected by sloppy writing. The same goes for poor grammar and bad spelling.

Should I try to impress the testgrader?

No. Don't forget that graders read dozens of essays at a time. They know a "snow job" when they see one. The only way to impress the grader without being phony as a wooden nickel is to use one of the instructor's pet ideas.

What do you mean by pet ideas?

Most instructors will have a handful of theories or approaches that they use again and again. It can be helpful if you are aware of these ideas to try to work them into your essay somehow. Of course, accuracy is essential. Don't push your luck!

Aren't most test-graders impressed with complex ideas?

Perhaps. But these difficult ideas shouldn't be difficult to read. Some of the world's most complex notions can be expressed in simple, straightforward language. Make an effort to simplify the complex. It's bound to win you points.

The Content of an Essay Answer

How long should my introduction be?

Even one word is too long for an essay introduction. As a rule, essays shouldn't have introductions. They only serve to cloud the focus of your answer.

How do I come up with a strong focus?

You can come up with a strong focus by answering the question in the very first sentence. The rest of the essay will then be developed from this opening sentence. The sentences which follow will be used to support the ideas and details which lead to your one sentence answer. Sound difficult? It's easy! The answer you just read is a good example. Reread it and you'll see.

Won't it "jump the gun" if my answer comes in the first sentence?

Not at all. Besides, if you don't answer right away you run the risk of finishing the essay without getting a shot off at all. Put your fire power in the very first sentence. That way you can be sure that you'll stick to the subject for the entire essay. [See Figure 10.2]

Does the first-sentence rule apply to long essays as well?

If your essay is several paragraphs long, put the answer in the first paragraph.

Wouldn't it be better to save the best for last and put the answer near the end of the essay?

That's a risky idea. Your instructor needs to know what you're getting at right away. You're writing an essay, not a mystery story. Your motives should be absolutely clear.

Figure 10.2 Answer the question in the very first sentence.

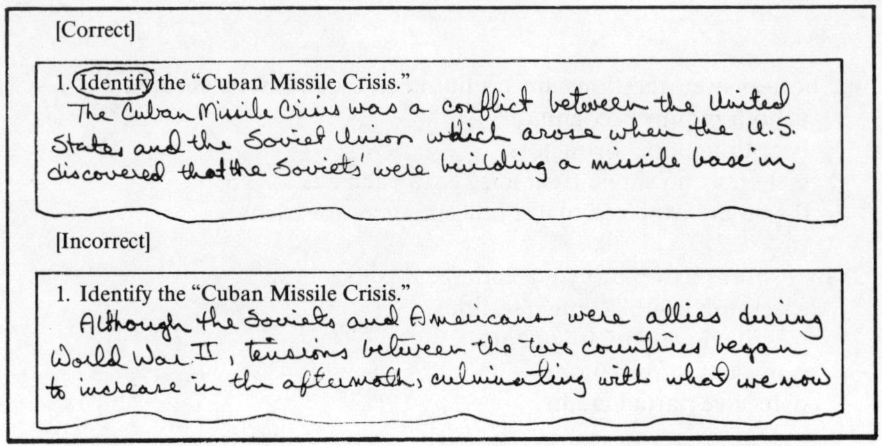

How should I end my essay then?

End your essay with a summary or repeat of the points that you made in your first sentence or paragraph.

Any final advice?

Yes, here are some hints that you should keep in mind on every essay test:

FIVE HINTS FOR TAKING ESSAY TESTS

1. **Use ink--**Pencil is not appropriate for an essay exam.

2. **Use only one side of each sheet--**This will prevent the previous page from showing through. It will also give you room for insertions, if you need them.

3. **Leave a generous lefthand margin--**Your paper will look neater and the grader will have room for comments.

4. **Leave spaces between your answers--**This will provide room in case you want to add to your answer later.

5. **Watch the time--**If it runs out unexpectedly, outline the points that you were planning to make. If you have extra time, go back and checkover your answers.

MULTIPLE-CHOICE QUIZ

1. Short-answer questions are similar to essay questions because
   a. both require recognition.
   b. both include distractors.
   c. there is no single right answer in each case.
   d. you are expected to use full sentences for each.

2. In a short-answer test your main goal is to
   a. rethink troublesome questions.
   b. write down any fragments.
   c. present information.
   d. receive partial credit.

3. The main thing which separates essays from short answers is
   a. tone.
   b. length.
   c. importance.
   d. all of the above.

4. The first thing you should do when you receive your essay exam is
   a. empty your mind.
   b. budget your time.
   c. read all the questions.
   d. read the directions.

5. Vague essay answers are usually the result of
   a. misunderstanding.
   b. poor writing skills.
   c. vague questions.
   d. a lack of time.

6. The most important feature of an essay answer is probably
   a. neatness.
   b. length.
   c. completeness.
   d. grammar.

7. Essay answers should follow the rule of
   a. "style before content."
   b. "one idea–one paragraph."
   c. "one idea per essay."
   d. "length before breadth."

8. In an essay, accepted opinions should be
   a. supported.
   b. your own.
   c. footnoted.
   d. avoided.

9. In an essay answer, the introduction should be
   a. brief.
   b. thorough.
   c. provocative.
   d. omitted.

10. The first sentence of your essay should
    a. restate the question.
    b. answer the question.
    c. provide a focus.
    d. all of the above.

11
BUILDING YOUR VOCABULARY

I'm not too concerned about my vocabulary, I don't plan on being a writer or speaker.

No matter where your interests lie, you should be concerned about your vocabulary if you want to be successful at what you do.

You mean there's a connection between vocabulary and success?

Definitely. A number of studies have reached this conclusion. Here are two of them.

Vocabulary and Success

A survey in an eastern engineering college showed that students who improved most in vocabulary during their freshman year averaged three or four places nearer the top of their class in academic standing during the sophomore year; those who did not improve at all in vocabulary averaged 7.5 places nearer the bottom.

The Human Engineering Laboratory, a company that specializes in testing business executives, found a very significant correlation between high vocabulary scores and success at the top executive level.

Even so, I don't want to learn a lot of long and difficult words. I'm, just interested in speaking precisely.

If you're interested in speaking precisely, you should be interested in building your vocabulary. A good vocabulary doesn't always mean a long and confusing one. Building your vocabulary will make you a clearer speaker. It will also enable you to read, and learn and even *think* more clearly.

But I think in concepts, not words.

Many people wrongly assume this. J.B. Watson, a noted psychologist has asserted that thinking is silent speech. In other words, when you think you do the same thing you do when you speak, only silently. In fact, studies have shown that thinking is accompanied by slight movements of the lips and other speech muscles. What this means then is that if your vocabulary is limited or imprecise your thinking will be as well.

OK, so what do I need in order to build my vocabulary?

The most important tool for vocabulary building is a dictionary.

Wouldn't a vocabulary book be better?

Vocabulary-building books may try to tell you how to increase your word power but, as we'll see, the methods they support aren't always successful. A good dictionary and a genuine interest in learning are much better bets.

Is an interest all that important?

Yes. Interest provides motivation; and motivation will put your plans into action.

How do I develop a genuine interest in words?

For many people an interest in words just comes naturally. But if that natural interest hasn't happened to you, you can create one by reading or just looking through any of a number of books about word origins. Once you learn a few of the fascinating origins of words, you'll find that you are curious about the roots of other words.

Can you give me an example?

Sure. Read this.

If You Love Your Glove

Anyone who takes good care of a baseball glove has heard of *neatsfoot oil*. Yet few people know the origin of this trusty oil's name. Despite what you may think, neatsfoot has nothing to do with the fact that this popular glove lubricant can also be used to keep a pair of leather shoes looking nice. The key to the mystery of neatsfoot oil lies in a meaning for *neat* that we no longer use. Up until the late nineteenth century the word *neat* referred to any animal of the bovine family, that is cows and oxen. Not surprisingly, the oil that ballplayers swear by is made by boiling the shin bones and feet of cattle.

Once I've got a dictionary and an interest in words how can I improve my vocabulary?

Your best bet is the *FRONTIER VOCABULARY SYSTEM,* developed by Johnson O'Connor. That's because the Frontier System is based on natural learning processes.

Do you mean that my vocabulary will increase naturally as time goes on?

No. That's another misconception. If you leave your vocabulary to build itself there's a good chance that it will get smaller instead of larger.

Well then, how does the Frontier System work?

From his research O'Connor has concluded that in learning words, as in most skills, we progress from the simple to the difficult in an orderly sequence.

Does that mean we learn short words first and long words later?

Not exactly. The difficulty of a word doesn't depend on its length. Nor does it hinge upon its frequency of use, its geographic origin, or its pronounciation.

What does make a word difficult then?

It is the complexity of the ideas behind the word which makes it difficult. Since words stand for ideas these ideas must be learned before the words can be understood. Simple synonyms just won't do.

How does the Frontier System help us to learn the complex ideas we need to know in order to learn complex words.

The Frontier System works by building on words that are already familiar to us so we can gradually move into the area of words that were once unfamiliar.

So that's where the "frontier" in the Frontier System comes from.

That's right. You can divide all of the world's words into three areas or zones. There is the zone of known words and the zone of unknown words. At the edge of the zone of known words is a third zone. This is your frontier. Edgar Dale calls it your *twilight zone.* That's because these words are known, but not yet mastered.

What is the importance of the twilight zone?

This is where the real learning takes place. The important thing about the words in the twilight zone is that they are to some extent familiar.

You may be able to pronounce them or perhaps you can even use them in a sentence. Yet, you still haven't been able to master their meaning. Normally, all that is necessary is a slight straightening out before these words become familiar.

How do I master the meanings of the words in the twilight zone?

That's where the dictionary comes in. You can find your word's precise meaning and usage in the dictionary. In time it will become one of your known words.

Can't I just skip the Twilight Zone and go straight into the zone of unknown words?

That's a bad idea. Even the slightest bit of familiarity with a word can help you to learn and remember its meaning. That familiarity provides you with a handle. When you skip right to the zone of unknown words there is nothing for you to grab onto; you have no connection with the words you encounter. As a result, learning becomes inefficient and often breaks down. This is the problem with many vocabulary-building books. They try to teach you words that are completely unknown to you.

Figure 11.1   The Frontier System

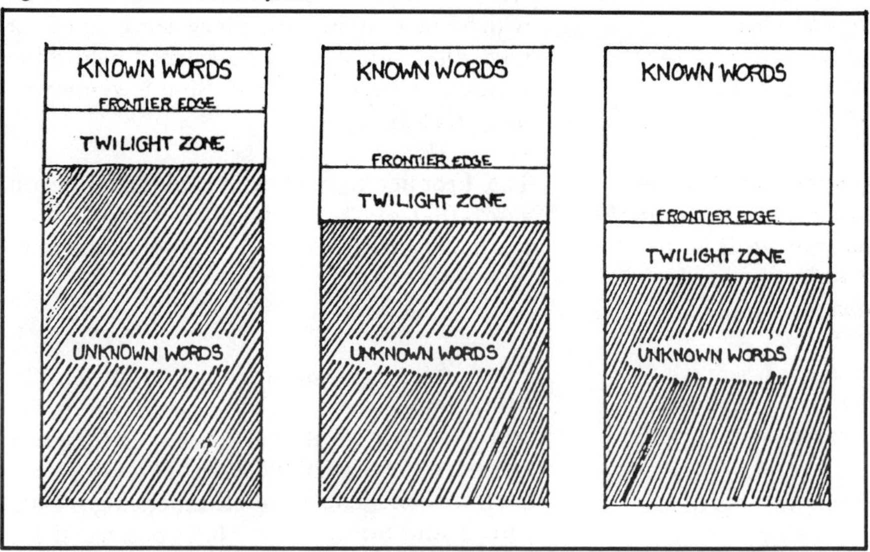

Yes, but don't they often teach me the words that I should know?

Words you should know are of no help if you are unable to master them. Furthermore the words in the twilight zone are just as important to know and much easier to learn.

What happens when I use up all of the words in my frontier zone?

Don't worry. That will never happen. As you learn more words the edge of your frontier will push further into the zone of unknown words. Your known words will increase and your unknown words will be reduced.

What frontier words should I begin with?

That really depends upon you. Everyone has a different frontier. One person's frontier word may be another's unknown or known word.

Yes, but aren't there some common frontier words?

There are at least some common categories that many of the frontier words fit into. Here are a few of them.

COMMON CATEGORIES FOR FRONTIER WORDS

1. **Words that sound somewhat alike.**
2. **Words that look somewhat alike.**
3. **Words that are used together.**
4. **Words that suggest an embedded word.**
5. **Words that set a prefix-root trap.**

1. WORDS THAT SOUND SOMEWHAT ALIKE.

Can you give me an example of two frontier words that sound alike?

Sure. How about *illicit* and *elicit?* If you know one of these words but not the other or if you know both of the words but get their meanings confused then you can consider them frontier words. *Illicit,* by the way, means "improper or unlawful." During Prohibition, selling alcohol was an *illicit* business. Elicit, on the other hand, is a verb which means "to draw out," as in "The teacher stood on his head just to see if he could elicit a response from the sluggish class."

A Switch-hitting Frog?

Baseball great Yogi Berra is notorious for his misuse of frontier words. Here's what he said about teammate Mickey Mantle:

> Mantle can hit just as good right-handed as he can left-handed. He's just naturally *amphibious.*

Amphibious means "able to live both on land and in the water."

What Yogi meant was *ambidextrous* which means "able to use both hands equally well."

The remark didn't even elicit a croak from Mantle, who by then was quite accustomed to his teammate's unique use of the English language.

2. WORDS THAT LOOK SOMEWHAT ALIKE.

What are two words that look something alike?

Martial and *marital* are two words that look quite a bit alike that you don't want to confuse. *Martial* means "pertaining to war or the military" as in *"martial* law" while *marital* means "pertaining to marriage" as in *"marital* bliss."

3. WORDS THAT ARE USED TOGETHER.

What do you mean by words that are used together?

There are a number of words that are used so often in pairs that we seldom see them by themselves. As a result we often draw the wrong conclusion about their meanings.

Can you give me an example?

Sure. In fact, I'll give you several.

Words That Are Used Together

Pair	Incorrect Meaning of Italic Word	Correct Meaning
prodigal son	Wandering	Wasteful; a spendthrift
exotic flower	Beautiful	Introduced from a foreign country
capital crime	Important	Punishable by death

4. WORDS THAT SUGGEST AN EMBEDDED WORD.

What's the problem with words that suggest an embedded word?

Words like *succulent, ramify* and *strident* all suggest embedded words. *(suck, ram* and *stride)* Yet none of them comes close to the meanings of the words they suggest. *Succulent* has nothing to do with sucking; it means juicy. To *ramify* something does not mean that you butt it with a log, medieval style. It means to divide or spread out into branches. Finally, *strident* has nothing to do with a runner, unless of course that runner has an unpleasant voice; it means harsh-sounding or shrill.

5. WORDS THAT SET A PREFIX-ROOT TRAP.

What is the prefix-root trap?

Those people who know something about prefixes and roots will sometimes push their knowledge a bit too far. For example, you may know that the words *bicycle* means "two wheels." So what does *biweekly* mean? Although it seems as though it should mean twice a week, the true meaning of *biweekly* is "every two weeks." The same goes with *sublime* which sounds like it means something underground when in fact its actual meaning is almost the opposite. *Sublime* means "elevated or exalted; noble."

You've provided me with a handful of possible frontier words. How can I find more?

Keep your ears and eyes open. That's the best way to spot frontier words. Listen to your own speech and take note of some of the more unusual words that you use. Are you certain of their definitions? Do the same with other people's conversations. You might be surprised to find that they aren't using some words properly. In reading, be on the lookout for words that you commonly run into but seldom use in conversation or in your own writing.

There are probably dozens of words that I run into in books that I don't use myself. Should I try to learn the meanings of all of them?

No. Remember the importance of interest in vocabulary building. Learn only the words that truly interest you, the words that you would like to become part of your vocabulary. Finally, after you've mastered some frontier words you might try learning their opposites. Learning pairs of contrasting words creates the strong force of spontaneous suggestion. From then on, whenever you use one of the words you'll think of its opposite as well.

After I've found my frontier words, what do I do with them?

Instead of writing out your frontier list on a single sheet of paper, it's better to put each word on a separate file card.

Figure 11.2   Writing Your Own Frontier Cards

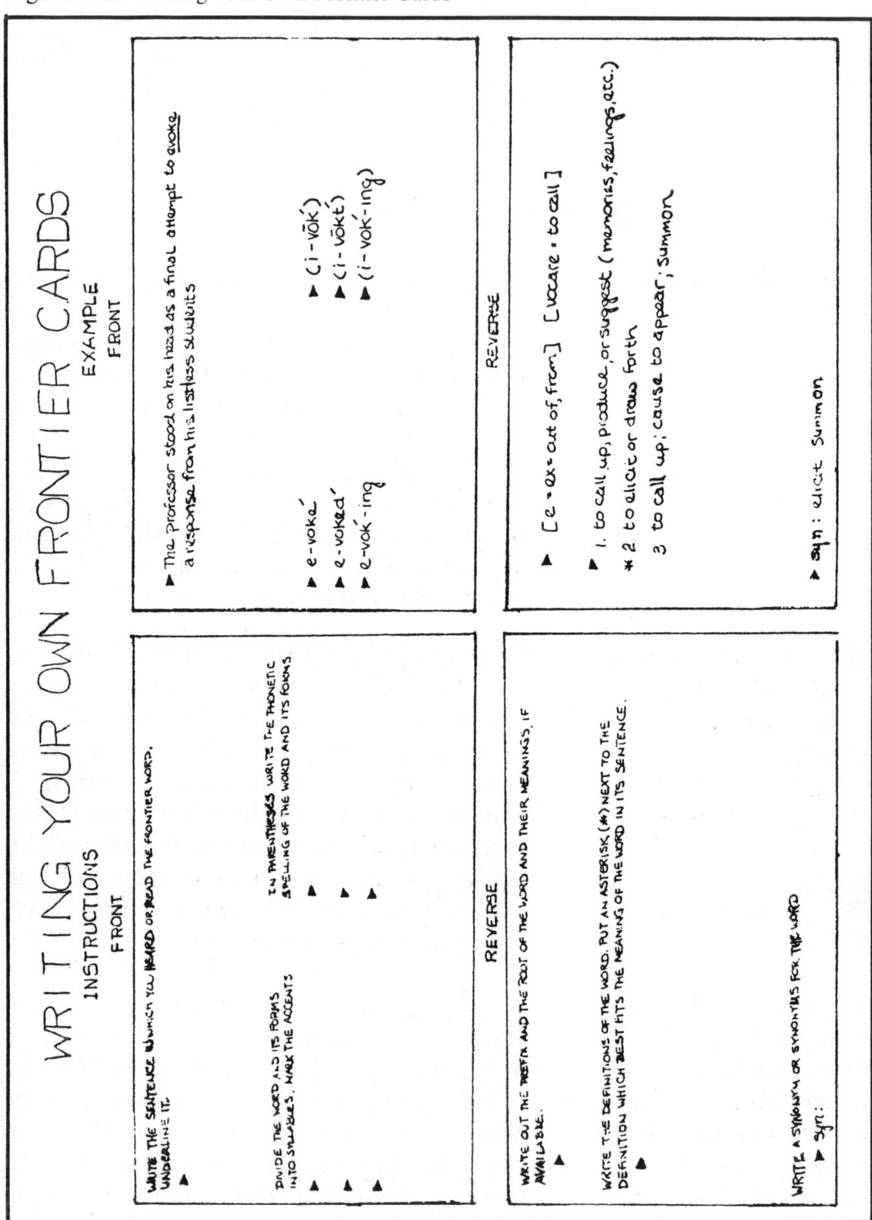

So I just write the word on a file card and that's it?

No, that's only the beginning. First of all, if you can, write the sentence in which you first encountered the word. Underline the word you're trying to learn so it will stand out. When you've gotten a small stack of these cards, head for the nearest unabridged dictionary.

Will a desk dictionary do?

If you have no other choice, yes. However, most college libraries have at least one unabridged dictionary. Many have several of these mammoth volumes per floor. By using an unabridged dictionary you'll be able to get the full story of the word in question. If you have to use an abridged dictionary you must sacrifice part of the story.

Just what is a word's full story?

Its pronunciation, its prefix and root, and all of its definitions.

Is the word's pronunciation that important?

Yes it is. Even if you only use the word in your writing you'll feel more confident when you know how it should be pronounced. And of course, in speaking, the correct pronunciation is essential. You'd be surprised at the number of people who go through life mispronouncing words when the correct pronunciation is as close as their nearest dictionary.

Where should I put the word's pronunciation?

On the front of the card, below the sentence in which you encountered the word. Divide the word into syllables and include all of its diacritical marks. Do the same with the other forms of the word that are included in the definition.

Some words can be pronounced in several ways.

You might want to write down all of the pronunciations just so you are aware of them. The first is usually the preferred.

What's the point of writing out a word's prefix and root?

Knowing a word's derivation can often tell you things about the word that you might not have learned from its definitions. For example, most of us know that a sophomore is a second-year student. But if you look at the derivation of the word you'll find that it comes from the two Greek words, *sophos,* meaning wise or clever and *moros* meaning foolish or silly! Apparently, the Greeks felt that second-year students were both educated and naive. Thus, they were wise fools. If you remember your sophomore year in high school, you'll see there's some truth in that.

Where do I find this information in the dictionary entry?

Information about a word's prefix and root is often enclosed in brackets and it usually comes after the definitions.

Where should I write the word's prefix and root on the file card?

That can go on the back of the card at the top.

How about the definitions?

You can put them just below the derivation.

Should I include all the definitions or just the one that describes the meaning of the word as I want to use it?

Include all the definitions but put an asterisk next to the one that fits the meaning of the word as it was used in your sentence. Some time you may want to learn the word's other meanings.

How do I study my Frontier cards?

Carry about a dozen of them around with you so you can review them whenever you have a bit of spare time. They're great to have around when you're waiting in line or taking a short bus trip. Grab one card at a time and look at the front side. Read the sentence completely, pronounce the word correctly, and then see if you can define it. Try and use your own words instead of dictionary language.

When do I use the back of the card?

After you've defined the word to the best of your ability flip the card over and check your definition with the definition that you've already written down. If you've defined the word accurately, move on to the next card. If not, flip back to the front of the card and put a dot in the upper right-hand corner.

What does the dot do?

It will remind you that you missed on a previous try. If a card gets three or more dots it's time to give that word some extra attention.

After I've mastered my stack of cards can I throw them away?

No. Place them in a file box and grab another small stack of cards that needs to be mastered. From time to time you may want to refer to your file box and review those words that you've already mastered.

Does the frontier system apply to the words or terms I learn in lectures and in my textbook?

Not exactly. The difference is that words and terms from textbooks and lectures have to be learned cold whether you like it or not. It would be a great mistake not to learn the precise meaning of such words. You might lose a few points on an exam or perhaps even jeopardize your overall understanding of the course.

So how do I learn these words?

Follow the same procedure that you used for your frontier words. Although you may not be as interested in these words at first, once you have an understanding of their precise meanings the words and the class from which they came may become more exciting to you.

T N' T: TIPS AND TECHNIQUES FOR MORE INFORMATION ON WORDS

1. Read books about words origins.
2. Learn prefixes and roots

1. Read books about word origins.

What book would you recommend if I wanted to learn more about the origins of words?

My personal favorite is a book called *Picturesque Word Origins,* published by Merriam-Webster, Inc. Its filled with fascinating explanations and interesting illustrations for the histories of common words like *bribe* and *rehearse.* Unfortunately, *Picturesque Word Origins* was published quite some time ago (1933) so it's no longer in print. However, you may be able to hunt up a copy at your local library or even at a used book sale. Believe me, it's worth looking for. Of course, there are quite a number of other books that have been written on the histories of words. Here's a short list of some of the books that should still be available.

Books on Words and Word Origins

Ciardi, John, *A Browser's Dictionary and Native's Guide to the Unknown American Language.* Scranton, PA, Harper & Row Publishers, Inc., 1980. The author discusses about a thousand words, including *baker's dozen* and *swindle.*

Funk, Charles E., *A Hog on Ice, and Other Curious Expressions,* Scranton, PA, Harper & Row Publishers, Inc., 1948. The author discusses about 750 phrases, such as *kick the* bucket and *kangaroo court.* Some illustrations or drawings.

Holt, Alfred H., *Phrase and Word Origins,* New York, Dover Publications, Inc., 1961. The author discusses over one thousand words and phrases from *armed to the teeth* to *wet your whistle.*

Laird, Charlton, *The Word: A Look at the Vocabulary of English,* New York, Simon and Schuster, Inc., 1981. How words enter and leave our language.

Maleska, Eugene, *A Pleasure in Words,* New York, Simon and Schuster, Inc., 1981. A look at the origins and meanings of thousands of words in our language by a distinguished educator, author, and current crossword puzzle editor of *The New York Times.*

Mathews, Mitford M., *American Words,* New York, Philomel Books, 1976. The author discusses about two hundred words such as *podunk* and *hickory,* and many are illustrated by drawings.

Shipley, Joseph T., *Dictionary of Word Origins,* Totowa, NJ, Littlefield, Adams & Co., 1979. The author discusses about two thousand words such as *arsenic, assassin,* and *whippersnapper.*

Train, John, *Remarkable Words with Astonishing Origins.* New York, Crown Publishers, Inc., 1980.

---

2. *Learn about prefixes and roots.*

I thought you said that it was a bad idea to learn prefixes and roots?

It is if you plan to use them instead of the dictionary. A number of the most common prefixes have several different meanings and so if you relied on them without the aid of a dictionary you could wind up very confused. However, prefixes and roots can help you to acquire a more precise meaning of certain words. They can also lead you to an understanding of a whole family of words. For example, the root word "voke" which comes from *voc* (to call), can help you to understand the precise meanings of quite a number of other words, all of which come from this same root.

Figure 11.3   A Constellation of Words from a Single Root

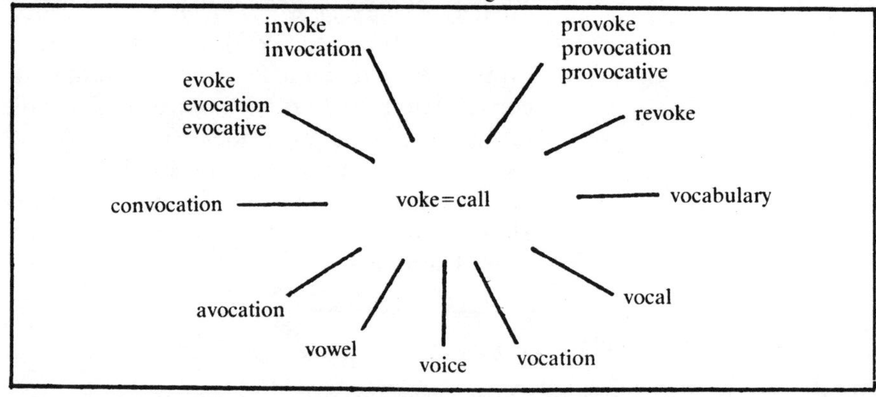

So, by all means, learn as many common prefixes and roots as you can. Just be sure not to use them as a dictionary substitute.

MULTIPLE-CHOICE QUIZ

1. A number of studies have found a link between a good vocabulary and
   a. business sense.
   b. athletic ability.
   c. success.
   d. intelligence.

2. We think
   a. imprecisely.
   b. out loud.
   c. in concepts.
   d. in words.

3. A word's difficulty depends upon its
   a. length.
   b. pronunciation.
   c. frequency of use.
   d. complexity of ideas.

4. The Frontier System works by building on words that are
   a. easy to pronounce.
   b. already familiar.
   c. complex.
   d. foreign.

5. As you master new words,
   a. your frontier zone decreases.
   b. your unknown words increase.
   c. your known words increase.
   d. all of the above.

6. A good way to accumulate Frontier words is to
   a. keep your eyes and ears open.
   b. use vocabulary-building books.
   c. borrow a friend's list.
   d. skim through a scholarly textbook.

7. In addition to the frontier word itself, you should also make note of
   a. the page on which the word was found.
   b. the sentence in which the word occurred.
   c. any homonyms the word may have.
   d. your guess of the word's definition.

8. As you review your Frontier words, it is important to define each one
    a. in your own words.
    b. silently.
    c. with dictionary language.
    d. approximately.

9. Old frontier cards should be
    a. marked with a dot.
    b. thrown away.
    c. mixed in with new cards.
    d. reviewed from time to time.

10. It is best to use prefixes and roots
    a. instead of the dictionary.
    b. along with the dictionary.
    c. when precision is not important.
    d. when the word is in Greek.

12
RESEARCH PAPERS

What's the toughest part about writing a paper?

Getting up enough nerve to start it. Papers, particularly research papers, strike fear into the hearts of most students, mainly because the task is unfamiliar. When the job becomes familiar, the assignment is a lot less frightening.

Is writing a paper like anything that we've already discussed?

Actually it is. Writing a research paper at least is like studying your notes. The only difference is that instead of reciting what you learn you write it instead.

What are the different types of papers that are commonly assigned?

Here's a list of the four most common paper assignments.

THE FOUR MAIN TYPES OF PAPERS

1. **The Theme:** This is a popular one in English courses. Themes are fairly short. They usually contain your own conclusions based on something that you have experienced, or more often, read.

2. **The Report:** This type of paper is used most often in the sciences. The form is generally dictated by the instructor and the content provides a discussion of the results of some sort of factual research.

3. **The Critical Essay:** Another favorite in English or other literature courses, it normally calls for your opinion on a piece of writing, usually a book.

4. The Research Paper: Longer than the other three, the research paper is based on extensive research from published material on a particular subject. The subject may be chosen by you in some cases, or in others, by the instructor.

What is the hardest paper to write?

Probably the research paper, only because it involves far more library work than the others. Otherwise, the writing of a research paper is pretty much the same as writing any other paper. For that reason, let's focus our discussion on the research paper.

How long does it usually take to write a research paper?

Weeks, months and even years have been spent on a research paper. The sad fact is that far too many students try to do the job in just a few days.

When should I begin writing then?

Start working on your paper just as soon as it is assigned. You wouldn't sit twiddling your thumbs through the first half of an exam and then begin answering questions. So, when you're given the time, make good use of it!

CHOOSING AND NARROWING YOUR TOPIC

What's the most crucial part of writing a research paper?

Choosing a topic. Everything hinges upon this. Hard work and good writing can be lost if you don't take the time to choose your topic carefully.

So how do I go about choosing a topic?

You can begin by picking a subject that interests you. There's nothing that says research papers have to be boring. An interesting topic can turn a chore into an adventure.

But what if the subject is assigned by the instructor?

The subject may be assigned but you can probably pick your own topic. You can often write about a subject that doesn't interest you but in an area that does.

Do you think I'll need to narrow my subject?

Almost definitely. The most common complaint from instructors is that the research papers are too broad.

112

How do I go about doing the narrowing?

It's a three step process. The idea is to take your topic and narrow it by one degree. Then take the narrowed topic and narrow it some more. Do this once more and you should have a topic that's neither too narrow nor too broad. [See Figure 12.1]

What happens after I've narrowed my topic?

It's time to do a little preliminary research. Your purpose is to see whether your narrowed topic has enough information to make a paper.

Where do I go for references?

The *Reader's Guide to Periodical Literature* is your best bet. Found in the library, it contains a listing of most of the articles which have appeared in major magazines since World War I.

What if I can't find enough articles on my subject?

That's why this research is only preliminary. If your topic doesn't seem to have enough articles, you still have a chance to change it.

Figure 12.1   Narrowing a paper topic.

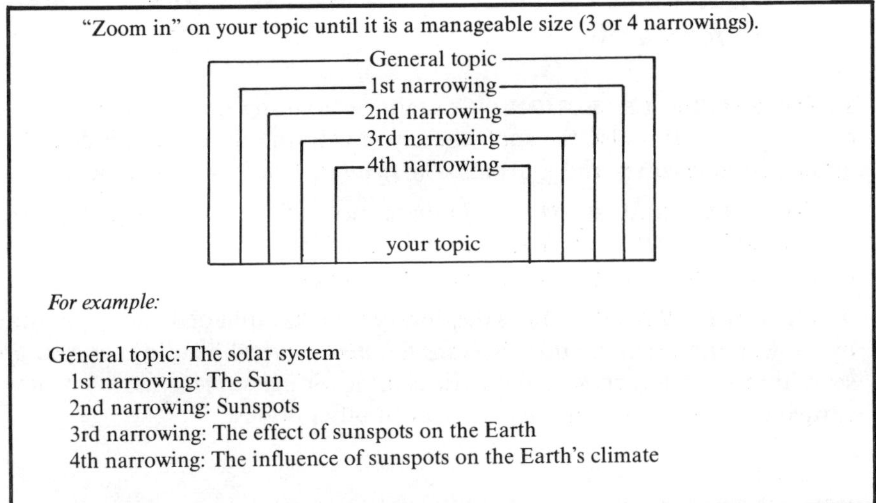

PROVIDING A FOCUS

And if I do find enough articles, what next?

Congratulations! You're ready to provide a focus for your subject.

What do you mean by a focus?

The world's most interesting topic is just a collection of facts unless it poses a critical question. That question will give your paper the purpose and direction it needs in order to be interesting. What's more, it should make researching a little easier for you. Although it is important to try to answer your question, don't feel as though you've failed if you can't. The pursuit of the answer is really more important than the answer itself. For an example question, see Figure 12.2.

Are personal opinions permitted in a research paper?

Yes they are, but don't get carried away. Your primary goal is to be informative, not judgmental.

DOING THE RESEARCH

Three Places to Head When You Need to Do Research

1. THE REFERENCE SECTION: Contains everything from phone books to encyclopedias. It is also the spot where you will find the current indexes for articles in magazines and journals. *The Reader's Guide* is located here.

2. THE PERIODICAL SECTION: Houses most of the library's newspapers and magazines. After you've collected the titles of possible sources (from the reference section) the periodical section is the place to go.

3. THE CARD CATALOG: Lists the library's books alphabetically, by author, by subject and often, by title. Be sure to check several headings as you are searching for references in the card catalog. Some subjects may not have earned their own book but may appear in other books.

What will I need in order to do research?

You'll need lots of index cards or, if you want to save some money, use 3 x 5 slips of paper. You'll be taking two sets of notes, one set for your bibliography, using one card for each source, and the other for your detailed notes. Although this may all seem time consuming, in the long run you'll be saving time.

Figure 12.2   Provide a focus.

> Give your paper direction and purpose by arriving at a question for your facts to answer.
>
> Your topic: *The influence of sunspots on the Earth's climate*
>
> Your focus-providing question: *Can sunspots have a devastating effect on the Earth's climate?*

How does writing up these bib slips save me time?

A bibliography is a requirement for almost all research papers. If you haven't written bibliography cards, you're going to have to return to the library and hunt down all of your sources for a second time. If you have been keeping a file of bib cards your job is a simple one, just a matter of transferring the information from your cards to your paper.

Is there a special form I should use for writing out a bib card?

Yes Here it is.

THE FORMAT OF THE BIBLIOGRAPHY CARD
The front of the card

Library Name	Brief Title of Your Subject
Library Call no.	Reference information in proper bibliographical form

What goes on the back of the bib card?

Save the back for any personal opinions you might have about the reference. If you like it, say so. If not, then explain why. This little bit of information will serve as an excellent way of refreshing your memory.

How should my note cards be written?

Each card should contain an abbreviation for the work it came from (or the author's name) as well as a page number. Write only one note per card. [See Figure 12.3]

Why only one note per card?

Although it may sound wasteful, writing one note per card should save hours of time that would have been spent in organizing your paper. Because each card contains only a single thought you can actually "write" your paper simply by arranging your cards in the order you want.

Figure 12.3   An example of 3 x 5 note slip.

Eleven Hints For Taking Notes

1. Use only one side of each slip for taking notes.
2. Identify the reference you used on each slip by writing the author's name or the book's title in the top left corner.
3. Write the page number where the note came from in the lower right.
4. Be sure to skim the article or chapter before you begin to take notes.
5. Write the notes in your own words. Not only will you understand them better but you will also get a headstart on the actual writing of the paper.
6. Make your notes brief but detailed enough to provide accurate meaning.
7. Write neatly so you won't have to "translate" later.
8. Use ink. Notes taken in pencil are apt to blur with time.
9. Keep your direct quotations to a minimum. Most students tend to overdo it when it comes to quotations.
10. Abbreviate only the common words so you can be sure of what you've written later on.
11. If an idea occurs to you while you're taking notes, put it on a separate slip with the caption "my own."

ORGANIZING YOUR PAPER

Do I have to write an outline?

Yes, but not right away. The first thing you want to do is to write down a list of the points that you'd like to cover in your paper. Use your slips for the information. Once you've accumulated the points you want from your slips, go back and decide which of these points you would consider to be major points and which ones would be minor points. You may also decide that some of these points are not useful. These should be aside. Don't try to work a point into your paper simply because it's interesting. Part of writing a paper involves knowing what to leave out.

What happens to the notes with minor points?

Go back and cluster them under the major points that they support. If they don't seem to support any of the major points then they probably don't belong in your paper. Once all of these minor points have been positioned, you'll have a primitive outline with major points and minor points. All you lack is organization.

How do I go about organizing my paper?

Organizing your paper involves asking yourself some hard questions: "Should I take a particular viewpoint?" "What should the basic theme of my paper be?" In other words "What do I want to say in my paper?" Once you can answer this, you're ready to choose an organizational pattern for your paper.

Which is the best organizational pattern for a research paper?

Pick a pattern which suits both the basic premise of your paper as well as your personal choice. Most college papers are written using the *time* or *process* pattern. In the time pattern your information follows a chronological order. In the process pattern steps or events are presented in a sequence that will lead to a desired situation or product. Another pattern you might try is *development of an argument* in which you state a premise and then use the rest of the paper to defend it.

What happens next?

Go back to the note slips, put them in the proper order and then number them from one to whatever. Then you can begin writing.

How do I start writing?

The best way to begin is by picking up your pen or pencil. Don't spend hours brooding over the perfect opening sentence. Just start writing! Go through your cards systematically, writing as rapidly and spontaneously as you can. You're not expected to come up with a masterpiece on the first try. Your goal for now is to write and keep on writing!

Should I start out with an introduction?

For now, one sentence will be sufficient. It's important to get right into the meat of the paper.

What about footnotes?

They can come later as well. In the meantime, whenever you use information from a reference be sure to write the number of the note card in parentheses at the end of the sentence so you won't be accused of plagiarism.

A FEW WORDS ABOUT PLAGIARISM

PLAGIARISM (using another person's words without acknowledgement) is stealing plain and simple. Words and ideas are personal property just like a car or a set of silverware. Using another person's writing even if you paraphrase it, is considered plagiarism.

You are foolish if you believe that you can get away with plagiarism. Everyone has a distinctive writing style and way of thinking. The instructor who is grading your paper is bound to notice any changes in either.

REWRITING AND EDITING

What happens after I've finished my first draft?

Go back and type up a clean copy and then set it aside for a day or two. This will give your paper a chance to "age" a little before you start on the next draft.

Why do I have to rewrite the paper before I put it aside?

Your rough copy is probably full of insertions and deletions. You may understand them all now but in two days they may make no sense at all. That's why it's important to "translate" your scribblings while you still understand them. Then when you come back to your paper you can begin editing it without delay.

What do you mean by editing?

Editing can mean rearranging a sentence, replacing an awkward word with a clearer one, checking to see that the paragraphs flow smoothly, even rewriting the paper from top to bottom. To be a good editor you need courage and concern, courage to face up to the fact that it may take hours of work to get your paper to sound the way you want it and concerned enough about the reader's reaction that you will make changes which will help to express your ideas as clearly as possible.

Are there some special things to look for when I'm editing?

Here are a couple of technical details that you should take care of.

FINE TUNING YOUR PAPER'S TECHNICAL DETAILS

The transitions--Don't make it obvious to the reader that your paper was written from one note slip to another. Try to make the shift from point to point smooth and easy to follow.

Grammar and spelling--Often underrated, these two elements of writing can make or break your paper. Errors in grammar and spelling may divert the reader's attention from the strength of your paper's content to the weakness of its style.

THE MISSING ELEMENTS

What's left to do in order to finish my paper?

Now's the time to fill in your paper's missing elements: footnotes, bibliography, the title, the introduction and the conclusion.

Do my footnotes have to go at the bottom of each page? That can be a real pain in the neck.

Your instructor may insist that you put your footnotes at the bottom of each page. If not, you have at least two other options: 1) You can put all of your footnotes together at the very end of the paper. (Be sure that you still put superscripts after every quoted or paraphrased line or paragraph.) 2) You can actually blend the footnotes right into the body of your paper. Each quoted or paraphrased line will be followed by parentheses which contain the author's name, the year the work was published and the page from which the information was taken. [See Figure 12.4]

Figure 12.4   Footnoting alternatives.

Credits known as "internal footnotes" can actually be included in the body of the paper. (Pauk, 1986, p. 00)

* * *

Another alternative is to put a superscript after each instance of quoted or paraphrased material and then put a complete listing of sources at the end of the paper.[1]

Notes

1. Walter Pauk, *Study Skills for Community and Junior Colleges,* (Clearwater: Reston-Stuart, 1987), p. 119.

2. Allan Paivio, *Imagery and Verbal Processes,* (New York: Holt, Rinehart and Winston, 1971), pp. 522-523.

What should I include in my bibliography?

The core of your bibliography should include all of the sources for your footnotes. In addition, you may include any published material that you have read as background for your paper.

Any advice on giving my paper a title?

Your title should reflect the content of your paper in some way. Although some students choose cute or amusing titles, don't feel that you have to be funny or tricky. A straightforward title is always your best bet.

Is now a good time to expand my introduction?

Use a general purpose statement as the foundation for your introduction. State your purpose and explain how you plan to carry it out.

What else should go in the introduction?

Sometimes an amusing anecdote or intriguing example can be a welcome addition to an introduction. Both can help to capture the reader's interest right from the start. But if the story doesn't seem to fit in naturally, don't force it. It's safer to write a straightforward introduction. No matter what you decide on, make an effort to link together your introduction, title and conclusion.

*What about the con-
clusion? Any special
recommendations for that?*

To begin with, make sure you have one. A paper without a conclusion will leave the reader dangling.

*What if my paper doesn't
need a conclusion?*

If your paper doesn't need a conclusion then you've got a problem with your organization. *All papers need conclusions.*

*Is the job of the conclusion
really to conclude?*

That's one of its roles. In addition, the conclusion will often be used to summarize or restate the paper's purpose. In that way it will link up with the introduction.

THE FINAL COPY

*Any special advice for the
final copy?*

You'd be surprised how many students ruin their hard work by cutting corners on the final copy. Normally the final copy is the only indication the instructor has of your effort. If it looks sloppy and disorganized your instructor may conclude that your overall work on the paper was sloppy and disorganized as well.. Don't leave that impression. Take the time to make your final copy look neat.

Seven Ways To Make A Good Paper Look Better

1. Use only one side of white paper.
2. Type your paper or have it typed. Double-space.
3. Leave ample margins to allow for the instructor's comments.
4. Erase your mistakes thoroughly. Don't use strikeovers.
5. Single space long quotations (five or more lines) indenting five spaces on each side. (There is no need for quotations marks with this format.)
6. Proofread carefully. Look for spelling errors, typos and other flaws.
7. Hand in your paper on time. A late paper will often lower your grade and start you off on the wrong foot.

MULTIPLE-CHOICE QUIZ

1. The most common complaint from instructors is that research papers are too
    a. broad.
    b. narrow.
    c. long.
    d. wordy.

2. Although an interesting topic is a good start, even the most fascinating subject requires a
    a. purpose.
    b. direction.
    c. critical question.
    d. all of the above.

3. A note card should *not* contain
    a. an abbreviation for the source that was used.
    b. the page number on which the note was found.
    c. the library call number of the book or article.
    d. a single thought or idea taken from the source.

4. Notes should be written
    a. neatly.
    b. in ink.
    c. in your own words.
    d. all of the above.

5. After you've written a "clean copy" of your first draft, it is important to
    a. go right to work on a second draft.
    b. give your paper a day or two to "age."
    c. go back and "translate" your scribblings.
    d. begin typing your footnotes.

6. Being a good editor requires
    a. courage.
    b. concern.
    c. a pen or pencil.
    d. all of the above.

7. Your bibliography should include
    a. footnote sources and published background material.
    b. only the sources you quoted from.
    c. only the sources you paraphrased.
    d. both quoted and paraphrased sources.

8. The foundation of your introduction should be
    a. your title.
    b. a general purpose statement.
    c. your first main idea.
    d. an amusing anecdote.

9. If your paper doesn't seem to need a conclusion
    a. simply restate your introduction.
    b. you don't have to include one.
    c. you have a problem with your organization.
    d. end with an interesting story or example.

10. Your final copy should be
    a. proofread carefully.
    b. typed double-space.
    c. handed in on time.
    d. all of the above.

ANSWERS TO CHAPTER QUIZZES

CHAPTER 1:   ACHIEVING SUCCESS

1. d	2. c	3. c	4. a	5. d
6. b	7. d	8. a	9. c	10. c

CHAPTER 2:   LEARNING TO CONCENTRATE

1. b	2. d	3. c	4. b	5. b
6. a	7. c	8. d	9. b	10. b

CHAPTER 3:   YOUR MEMORY

1. a	2. c	3. a	4. c	5. a
6. b	7. a	8. d	9. b	10. d

CHAPTER 4:   THE CORNELL NOTETAKING SYSTEM

1. d	2. a	3. d	4. d	5. b
6. c	7. a	8. b	9. c	10. d

CHAPTER 5:   CLASSROOM LECTURES

1. c	2. a	3. d	4. b	5. b
6. c	7. a	8. d	9. c	10. b

CHAPTER 6:   TEXTBOOK ASSIGNMENTS

1. a	2. c	3. d	4. d	5. b
6. c	7. b	8. c	9. d	10. b

CHAPTER 7:   PUTTING YOUR NOTES TO WORK

1. b	2. c	3. a	4. b	5. d
6. a	7. d	8. c	9. d	10. c

CHAPTER 8:   PREPARING FOR EXAMS

1. d	2. b	3. d	4. b	5. a
6. c	7. a	8. d	9. b	10. c

CHAPTER 9:   OBJECTIVE TESTS

1. a	2. b	3. c	4. a	5. d
6. c	7. c	8. d	9. b	10. c

CHAPTER 10:   ESSAY TESTS

1. c	2. c	3. b	4. a	5. a
6. c	7. b	8. a	9. d	10. d

CHAPTER 11:   BUILDING YOUR VOCABULARY

1. c	2. d	3. d	4. b	5. c
6. a	7. b	8. a	9. d	10. d

CHAPTER 12:   RESEARCH PAPERS

1. a	2. d	3. c	4. d	5. b
6. d	7. a	8. b	9. c	10. d